CHARLES DYER

WHAT'S NEXT?

GOD, ISRAEL AND THE FUTURE OF IRAQ

MOODY PUBLISHERS
CHICAGO

© 2004 by
CHARLES H. DYER

All rights reserved. No part of this book may be reproduced in any form without permission in writing from the publisher, except in the case of brief quotations embodied in critical articles or reviews.

All Scripture quotations, unless otherwise indicated, are taken from the *New American Standard Bible®*. Copyright © The Lockman Foundation 1960, 1962, 1963, 1968, 1971, 1972, 1973, 1975, 1977, 1995. Used by permission.

Library of Congress Cataloging-in-Publication Data

Dyer, Charles H., 1952
  What's next?: God, Israel, and the future of Iraq / by Charles H. Dyer.
      p. cm.
Includes bibliographical references.
  ISBN 0-8024-0907-5
1. Bible—Prophecies—Israel. 2. Bible—Prophecies—Iraq. I. Title.

  BS649.P3D94 2004
  220.1'5—dc22

                                2003025066

3 5 7 9 10 8 6 4 2
Printed in the United States of America

This book is dedicated to my dear friend, Dr. Mark Bailey, president of Dallas Theological Seminary. We share in common three great loves: God's Word, God's land, and God's people. And together we long for His Son's appearing. Maranatha!

CHARLES H. DYER

ACKNOWLEDGMENTS

Birthing a book is a collaborative effort, and I wish to acknowledge those whose assistance was an indispensible part of this project.

I want to start by thanking Betsey Newenhuyse for her wonderful editorial help. Her assistance in shaping the many disparate pieces into a coherent whole was invaluable.

Special thanks also goes to William Thrasher, Associate Publisher at Moody, for his persistence. This book exists because he refused to accept "no" for an answer.

I also want to thank the team at Moody Publishers who have done so much to package and promote the book. You are the ones who helped shape the words and JPEG files into such a visually attractive product—and who have helped others see its value. Janis, Dave, Rhonda, and John, I'll eat pizza with you any day!

Finally, I want to extend my special thanks to my dear friend Mark Tobey. You are a writer's dream—and your oversight made this project a reality.

CONTENTS

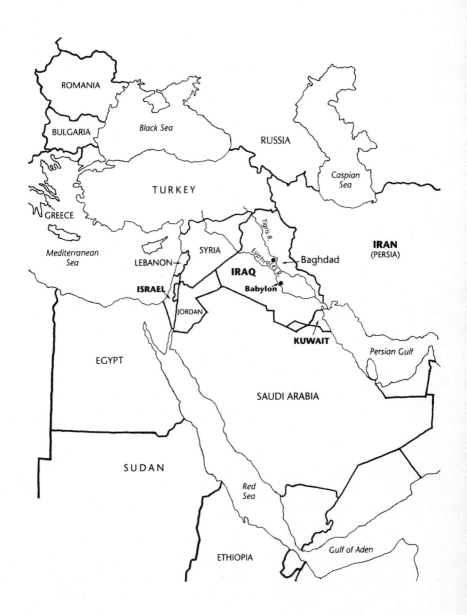

Prologue

See, I am doing a new thing! Now it springs up; do you not perceive it? I am making a way in the desert and streams in the wasteland.

Isaiah 43:19 NIV

Come to the wilderness.

Climb with me over the rough rocks to a spot where we can look out over the twisting valleys and the rugged mountains. Listen carefully to the wind whistling down through the canyons. With just a little imagination you can hear the sounds of a hundred generations being carried along on that wind—the breath of all the people who've ever lived in that land.

Here is the muted whisper of David, warning the others in hiding of Saul's approach. Here is the panting of Elijah, cowering under the broom tree after running the length of the land fleeing Jezebel. Here is the labored breathing of father Abraham, obeying his Lord to the point of making the most terrible of sacrifices. And here are the murmuring children of Israel as they gather the manna that dots the dry ground like an early November snowfall.

Here, finally, is the calm, but determined, voice of Jesus, who has left the Jordan River behind Him and journeyed alone into the wilderness, preparing to embark on His mission as Israel's Messiah—a mission that would ultimately lead Him to Calvary's cross. Satan, of course, knows this and tugs at Jesus, hoping to turn His heart. "Wouldn't You rather rule over all the nations right now? Imagine being ruler of all this! Here, aren't You hungry?" A sudden gust of wind reminds us of His resolve to follow God's will, revealed in His Word. "It is written. . . ."

Come with me to the wilderness, the place of testing —the place where God shows that He alone is sufficient. Here, perhaps, you will sense His presence, for the land has remained unchanged over thousands of years. The scene seems so peaceful . . . until you approach an army checkpoint where grim soldiers point a machine gun at you from behind concrete barriers.

Peace?

Now come with me to the water.

It's morning on the Sea of Galilee. We have chugged far enough out from shore that we can't see the power lines or the cars zipping by. We've cut the motor on the boat and rock gently, listening to the waves lapping against the sideboards. Overhead a gull wheels and screeches, seeking fish. The sun dances on the water. There's the faint, unmistakable smell of boat fuel.

And suddenly it hits us: Jesus was here. This is the place. This is what He saw, heard, felt. This was the lake where Peter, Andrew, James, John, and all the rest saw Him still the storm when He commanded the waves! "Peace! Be quiet!"

Peace?

At the top of the ridge, just to the east, are remains of Syrian bunkers where soldiers once took aim at Jewish farmers below. Syria is still demanding that the land be returned. Would such a move bring Israel closer to peace . . . or would it threaten her very existence?

Introduction
The Tortured Land

"It will come about in that day that I will make Jerusalem a heavy stone for all the peoples; all who lift it will be severely injured. And all the nations of the earth will be gathered against it."

Zechariah 12:3

Sadly, in this land that stirs the souls of so many —be they Christian, Jew, or Muslim—there is no peace, nor has there been peace for quite a long time. The Holy Land instead has witnessed some of the most unholy atrocities humanity can imagine. What is it about this relatively small piece of real estate that gives it such significance and stirs such passion?

Few of us can recall a time when headlines about the Middle East did not dominate the front pages and the evening news. The people, places, and events serve as mileposts along the highway of modern history. Moshe Dayan, the daring general with the eye patch, seemed to epitomize the brave pioneer spirit of the young nation Israel as he led the nation against its Arab neighbors in the Six-Day War of 1967. Henry Kissinger's "shuttle diplomacy" in the early 1970s defused a crisis that threatened to spark an international conflagration. Egypt's Anwar Sadat stunned the world and brought a ray of hope with his dramatic announcement: "I will go to Jerusalem!" Yitzhak Rabin, Yasser Arafat, and Bill Clinton shook hands at the White House, offering the world a brief glimmer of hope for peace.

Other images crowd in: the terror of the Munich Olympics in 1972. Angry Palestinians wearing black-and-white *kaffiyehs* to hide their faces, their clenched fists pounding the air as a symbol of Palestinian defiance. Children throwing stones. Buses blowing up. News stories every Christmas showing a tense Bethlehem patrolled by soldiers. Meanwhile, those of us reading and watching thousands of miles away wonder, *Why? What is this hatred that will not go away?*

Israel seems to be the epicenter of the events shaking the Middle East, but the aftershocks can be felt throughout the region. Still other images, other countries. In 1979 a cadre of grim, turbaned old men in beards encouraged young men in the streets of Tehran, Iran—a country most Americans struggled to locate on a map—to shout "Death to America!" and Ted Koppel became an overnight celebrity hosting a new program called *America Held Hostage*. For the first time many in America learned that this represented a fundamentalist strain of Islam—a religion with a billion or so adherents worldwide that most Americans vaguely associate with Arabs and deserts. But these old men weren't Arabs; they were Persians. And nearly a quarter of a century after this aftershock Iran joined the rulers of Iraq and North Korea in President George Bush's "axis of evil."

Confused by the multiplicity of people, nations, and events? It gets worse. In the oldest land of all, Iraq, not to be confused with Iran, a dictator named Saddam Hussein—not to be confused with King Hussein of Jordan—chose 1980 as the year both to begin rebuilding the ancient city of Babylon and to launch an attack against the Iranians that began an eight-year war of attrition that threatened to spread to all the nations of the Middle East. The ink was barely dry on the peace agreement between Iraq and Iran when Hussein decided to use chemical weapons against the Kurds in northern Iraq. Two years later Iraq's army invaded Kuwait and eventually confronted American power in 1991's Gulf War.

Ten years later, the Middle East came to America.

While the ruins of the World Trade Center smoked, we wept and wondered, *Why? Who are these people? Why do they hate us? And can it happen again?*

Which brings us to the present.

The "road map" for peace between the Israelis and Palestinians, a plan that raised the hopes of so many, seems destined to go the way of all the other peace plans advanced over the years, buried in the rubble of a score of bombed-out restaurants and the demolished homes of the suicide bombers. The United States struggles to rebuild Iraq in a murky state somewhere between settled peace and all-out conflict. Saddam Hussein, initially suspected of commanding a bloody Iraqi resistance from a series of safe houses and secret bunkers, was discovered by U.S. coalition forces cowering in a dank spider hole six feet beneath a sheep farm outside his hometown of Tikrit. Still, lurking in the back of many of our minds remains the fear that al-Qaeda or a similar group could strike again, perhaps unleashing a crude nuclear, biological, or chemical device in a major U.S. city.

I love the land of Israel and the other countries of the Middle East; I sorrow for them. Some of the people who live there are my personal friends. I have visited the Middle East over fifty times; Jerusalem is as familiar to me as the walk to my office in downtown Chicago. I'm well acquainted with the political ins and outs. I've studied the history. And I've listened to the people.

So what is next for this beautiful, tortured region, the area where God first strolled in the garden He had created, the stage on which God played out His biblical drama, the land where Jesus of Nazareth paid the ultimate price?

We might first ask, "What does *God* have planned for this region?" For the future of the Middle East is inextricably woven into God's plan for the final unrolling of history. In my book *The Rise of Babylon,* I looked at Saddam Hussein's efforts to rebuild the fabled city of Babylon (efforts I was invited to witness first-hand) and explored the role of that renascent city in earth's final drama. Here we will journey together through a larger territory, Bible in hand, seeing what God says about the future of the Middle East. I'll also share stories of a few people I have encountered in my travels, real people with real families and real struggles, people who daily live under the threat of violence. I will also try to connect some of the seemingly disparate dots of the Middle East puzzle. We will look at "Other Views" from a variety of perspectives on that puzzle. And, in the end, I will share why I think all these questions are much more than merely interesting information—they have urgent and eternal import.

Join me now as we look at the land, the people, and the future.

CHARLES H. DYER

1
Those Who Forget History . . .

If I forget you, O Jerusalem, may my right hand forget her skill. May my tongue cleave to the roof of my mouth, if I do not remember you, if I do not exalt Jerusalem above my chief joy.

Psalm 137:5–6

When I was a boy, I visited Gettysburg, Pennsylvania, and saw a diorama on the great battle that took place there, one of the decisive battles of the Civil War. I wasn't terribly impressed with the exhibit at the time, though; because, I thought, the battle had taken place so long ago. Who cares about something that happened a hundred years in the past? That's ancient history!

Many years later, when I was in Iraq, I was taken to a similar diorama commemorating the Battle of Qadisiyah. This battle depicted in the diorama, which celebrated the Arab Muslim victory over the Persians, took place in the seventh century (A.D. 637)—yet to the Muslim mind, it was still very real.

A while back there was a best-selling book titled *Don't Know Much About History* by Kenneth C. Davis. The title, pulled from a line in a 1960s rock song, described what is true of so many Americans: We don't know much about the past, and we don't really care. America excels at looking forward, not backward. But we forget the past at our peril. The Muslims of the Middle East have developed a far greater appreciation of history. They remember the glories. They also remember the injustices and the losses.

So before we reflect on "what's next" for the Middle East, it's helpful to think about how we got to where we are right now.

Toward a Jewish Homeland

The late nineteenth century saw a rise in anti-Semitism in Europe, exemplified by the famed trial of French army captain Alfred Dreyfus. Dreyfus, a Jew, was accused in 1894 of spying for Germany. He was convicted of the charges, partly on evidence forged by anti-Semitic officers, and sentenced to life imprisonment on the infamous Devil's Island. Eventually, he was exonerated of the charges . . . twelve years after the trial.

Theodor Herzl was a reporter for a Vienna newspaper who covered the Dreyfus trial. Herzl, who was Jewish, was troubled by the pervasive anti-Semitism he witnessed. He wrote a pamphlet in 1896 entitled *The Jewish State,* in which he argued for a homeland for the Jewish people. The first Zionist Congress was held in

Switzerland in 1897 to promote the formation of a Jewish state. (In biblical times Zion referred to the city of Jerusalem captured by David, who established it as the civil and religious center for the nation of Israel [Psalm 132:13–18].)

There was some debate over where the homeland should be established. Various options, including Uganda in Africa, were considered, but the heart of the Jewish people always returned to their ancestral homeland. Unfortunately, at the time, the area that is now the State of Israel was part of the Ottoman Empire and was under Turkish control. Though there had always been a Jewish presence in the land throughout the entire two thousand years of the Diaspora—and though by the turn of the century the majority population in Jerusalem was Jewish—much of the rest of the land was populated by Arabs. Still, the 1905 Zionist Congress decided that Palestine, the ancient cradle of the Jewish people, would once again be home to the people of the Diaspora, who had for centuries wandered stateless, forced to move from place to place in search of a welcome.

Religious persecution in Russia and Eastern Europe aided the Zionist cause. Thousands of Jews heeded the call to flee the pogroms of the czars and to return to the land of their forefathers. "Next year in Jerusalem!" became a rallying cry for increasing numbers of Jews seeking to make the journey to Palestine.

But this return was not without struggle. As the number of Jews living in Palestine rose, so did the level of opposition from the Arabs already living in the land. Though most of the new Jewish settlements were started on land purchased from Arab owners—uninhabited land that was often nothing more than mosquito-infested wetlands—the local natives still viewed the new settlements, and their advanced farming practices, with suspicion. A clash of cultures became inevitable.

Of course, had the movement to return to the land only been the vision of a small number of disenfranchised Jewish pioneers, the cultural clash might have resulted in nothing more than the destruction of these small communities at the hands of the local Turkish authorities. It was not enough for a group of Zionists simply to choose a country and move there. For the dream to succeed they needed the assistance of the major world powers. The "war to end all wars" provided the opportunity to obtain that assistance.

Dividing Up the Pie

During World War I, the Ottoman Empire, which controlled much of the Middle East, allied itself with the Central Powers—Germany and Austria. The strategic location of the Middle East—and the newly discovered oil wealth that fueled the automobiles, airplanes, and ships of the industrialized West—made the region crucial to the success of the war effort for both sides. If you've seen the film *Lawrence of Arabia,* you have an idea of how the British marshaled Arab support in the fight against the Turks. In that process, the British high commissioner in Egypt in 1916, Sir Henry McMahen, promised the Arab leadership postwar independence for all former Ottoman Arab provinces. "Help Britain defeat the Turks, and we will grant you independence and control over all Arab land."

In the meantime, Britain was working with chemist Chaim Weizmann, a Zionist, on developing a replacement for acetone, a substance critical to the war effort. In 1917 a grateful Arthur Balfour, the British foreign minister, committed Britain to work for "the establishment in Palestine of a national home for the Jewish people" in a letter that became known as the Balfour Declaration. To complicate matters further, in 1916 the British and French had signed the Sykes-Picot Agreement, which basically said, "When this is all over, here's how we're going to divide the Middle East between us."

Look at a map of the modern Middle East and you can see, in part, how the British and French carved up the remains of the Ottoman Empire, balancing their strategic interests against the various promises they made to different groups. They literally laid out a map, took a ruler, and said, "Here, your sphere of influence will extend over this area . . . but we want to control that area." And as they parceled out land to the different clans, those not receiving control over the Arabian Peninsula (with Mecca and Medina) were awarded Transjordan or Iraq. In large measure that was how several of the countries in the modern Middle East came to be.

Unfortunately, with the insensitivity the West can sometimes be guilty of, they often neglected natural tribal and clan divisions and created highly arbitrary boundaries. Those boundaries have created some lasting problems—including, eventually, the Gulf War, which was fought, in part, over territory between Iraq and Kuwait called "the disputed land," where a line on a map literally got smudged. That smudge happens to sit over an area awash in oil, so a mile in either direction could mean billions of dollars.

Back to the Land

Immediately after World War I, the flow of Jews into Palestine continued unabated, igniting even greater strife with the local Arabs. This strife played into the hands of despots like Hajj Amin al-Husseini, the Grand Mufti of Jerusalem. Most of the surrounding Arab countries were granted independence, but the land of Palestine remained under British control. As they administered this "Mandate," the British government tried to balance their competing promises to the Jews and the Arabs—allowing continued Jewish immigration but never following through on their promise to create a Jewish state. Husseini used the fear of a Jewish state to whip up the masses. They rioted against the Jews living in the land and against the British who were trying to administer the land. The flow of Jewish immigrants to Palestine dropped to a mere trickle, and it looked as if the dream of a homeland for the Jews would be but another of the broken promises from World War I.

The closing of Palestine to Jewish immigration moved from being a minor concern to a major catastrophe when Adolf Hitler came to power in Germany. Just when the Jewish people most needed a safe haven from a fanatical madman, the door for their escape was barred shut. Nearly six million Jews perished in Europe during the Holocaust. We will never know how many hundreds of thousands could have been saved had the British followed through on their pledge to create a homeland in Palestine for the Jewish people. Only after World War II did the world realize the enormity of this error.

The horrors of Hitler's program of genocide forced the world to acknowledge the need to provide a haven for the Jewish people. In 1947 the United Nations General Assembly voted to partition the former British Mandate into two states, Palestine and Israel. The plan was immediately rejected by the Arab nations. Then, on May 14, 1948, the Jewish leadership voted to establish the State of Israel. The declaration came into effect the following day as the last British troops withdrew. Palestinians remember May 15 as *al-Nakba,* or "the Catastrophe."

That's the key: "Palestinians remember." Imagine, for example, if in the year 2051 Americans still nursed bitter memories of September 11, 2001—memories so sharp and painful that all our foreign policy was built around avenging those attacks. As I write this, it is a mere two years after that dark day, yet the American people are already divided about how to pursue the "war on terror," how to balance national security with personal liberty, and to what extent we should commit to the rebuilding of Iraq. (Although, as we shall see, according to the Bible the rebuilding is a foregone conclusion—regardless of what the United States does or does not do.) The point simply is that we do not understand such grievances, such long memories. And we are paying the price.

What's Next?

The Arab world did not wait long to retaliate against the new State of Israel, even if it had the blessing of the United Nations. The day after the State of Israel came into being, five Arab armies from Jordan, Egypt, Lebanon, Syria, and Iraq attacked the fledgling nation but were repulsed. An armistice was eventually reached that established Israel's borders, which were larger than those initially agreed to by the Jewish people. Egypt kept the Gaza Strip, and Jordan annexed the West Bank.

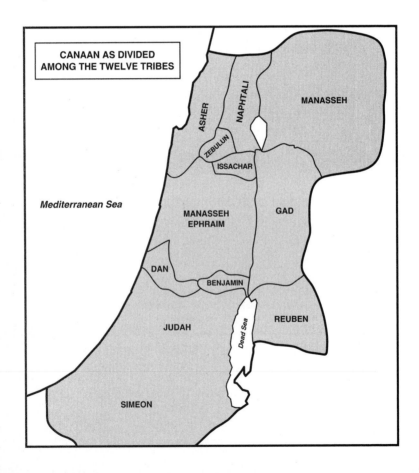

CANAAN AS DIVIDED AMONG THE TWELVE TRIBES

ASHER
NAPHTALI
MANASSEH
ZEBULUN
ISSACHAR
Mediterranean Sea
MANASSEH EPHRAIM
GAD
DAN
BENJAMIN
REUBEN
JUDAH
Dead Sea
SIMEON

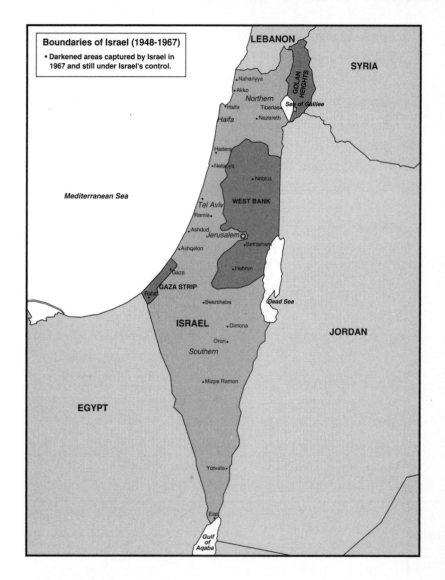

Boundaries of Israel (1948-1967)
• Darkened areas captured by Israel in 1967 and still under Israel's control.

War Without End

By 1967, tensions between Israel and its Arab neighbors had reached a boiling point, culminating in June's Six-Day War. Israel and her smaller but better trained military force captured the Gaza Strip and the Sinai from Egypt, the Golan Heights from Syria, and the West Bank from Jordan. Israel's stunning military victory gave the country borders that were easier to defend and a much larger geographical "buffer" where it could position its military hardware. Unfortunately, the war also placed Israel in control of the large Palestinian population centers in the West Bank and Gaza Strip—cities like Nablus, Jenin, Ramallah, Bethlehem, and Gaza City. Eventually these would prove to be hotbeds of deep hostility and conflict.

One of the other unexpected consequences of Israel's War of Independence in 1948 and the Six-Day War of 1967 was the creation of a great refugee problem. Hundreds of thousands of Arabs fled their homes during these periods of crisis. After Israel proved victorious in battle, many were unable to return home. What this meant in human terms was that upwards of eight hundred thousand Palestinians, a number comparable to a good-sized American city, lost their homes. Some had been told by the Arab nations, "Come away. When the battle's over you can go back and take the Jewish homes." Some fled out of fear; some were forced out by Israel, afraid of having enemies in its midst. Few ever returned.

A little-known sidelight to the conflict is the story of the nearly equal number of Jews who were forced to flee such Muslim countries as Egypt, Morocco, Tunisia, Iraq, and Iran, some with nothing but the clothes on their backs. The difference, however, is that Israel absorbed these refugees, who found homes and jobs and became productive members of Israeli society. The

Arab nations, despite their overtures to the Palestinians, isolated most of them in refugee camps where they lived in squalor for decades.

And so the "Palestinian problem," and its corollary, terrorism, has stymied and continues to stymie efforts on behalf of peace. In 1987 a mass uprising, or *Intifada*, swept Gaza and quickly spread to the West Bank—these are the familiar images of youths throwing rocks at Israeli soldiers on patrol and anti-Semitic graffiti scrawled across the iron doors of shuttered shops in the Old City of Jerusalem.

In 1991, the Gulf War opened a door for talks of peace. Following the expulsion of Iraq from Kuwait, Yasser Arafat lost the backing of the wealthy Gulf States because of his support for Saddam Hussein. The loss of financial support paved the way for secret negotiations to find a "final resolution" to the conflict between Israel and the Palestinians. Those negotiations climaxed in the famous handshake on the White House lawn on September 13, 1993, between President Clinton, PLO Chairman Yasser Arafat, and Israeli Prime Minister Yitzhak Rabin. Unfortunately, Rabin was assassinated in 1995, terrorist assaults increased, and the talks stalled.

In 2000 President Bill Clinton sought to push the talks forward to reach a final settlement on all remaining issues. At a marathon summit at Camp David the president presented a blueprint for resolution that included the establishment of a Palestinian state, the return of virtually all territory in the West Bank captured by Israel in 1967, and the complete recognition of Israel by the Palestinians. Though both sides initially agreed with the proposal, Yasser Arafat came back with additional demands related to the status of Jerusalem and the right of return of Palestinian refugees to Israel. Israel could not accept these additional demands, and the negotiations ended without agreement.

And Now?

The familiar cycle of violence had already resumed as the negotiations between the Israelis and the Palestinians grew ever more acrimonious. They escalated further when Ariel Sharon, leader of the Likud Party in Israel, toured the *Haram es-Sharif* (the Temple Mount complex) in Jerusalem in September 2000. Sharon's critics saw it as a highly provocative move. Palestinian demonstrations followed, quickly developing into what became known as the *al-Aqsa Intifada.* There have been moves toward establishing renewed negotiations with the Palestinian leadership—excluding Yasser Arafat— but every time agreements are reached, terrorist groups such as *Hamas* undermine the shaky steps toward peace.

This thumbnail history has skirted other countries of the Middle East and other issues. But, as we shall see, the question of Israel—the existence of Israel—lies near the heart of many of those other issues.

OTHER VIEWS

From the *Hamas* Manifesto

The land of Palestine is an Islamic *Waqf* [religious endowment] consecrated for future Muslim generations until Judgment Day. It, or any part of it, should not be squandered; it, or any part of it, should not be given up. . . . This is the law governing the land of Palestine in the Islamic *Sharia* [law], and the same goes for any land the Muslims have conquered by force, because during the times of conquests, the Muslims consecrated these lands to Muslim generations till the Day of Judgment.

2
Unraveling the Matrix

Just as you do not know the path of the wind and how bones are formed in the womb of the pregnant woman, so you do not know the activity of God who makes all things.

Ecclesiastes 11:5

I know a shopkeeper in Bethlehem. He's a Christian—not a believer in the evangelical sense, but a Christian as opposed to being Muslim or Jewish. He once was very prosperous, a multimillionaire. But the past two decades of struggles, and particularly the years since the pivotal year of 2000, have virtually wiped him out. My friend symbolizes the plight of Palestinian Christians caught between the warring sides. He has been attacked by Muslims and shaken down by the notoriously corrupt Palestinian Authority. He has suffered greatly under Palestinian rule.

Yet he continues to blame Israel.

In a revealing conversation I had with him while Bill Clinton was still president, he insisted that Israel hates the Arabs and the American president could force Israel to make peace, because America is all-powerful. So why does the strife continue? Why does Israel not make peace? Because, my friend said, America is actually controlled by Israel—by a Zionist secret society.

I finally said to him, "Come on, I live in America. The idea that the Jews secretly control America is just not true."

"Let's go through it," he responded, ticking off the ostensible proofs. "Secretary of State: Madeleine Albright. She's Jewish. Secretary of Defense: William Cohen, Jewish. Monica Lewinsky, Jewish. It's all a Zionist conspiracy."

That's a common sentiment among Arabs, whatever their religion. And it is accepted as virtually a pillar of truth among Muslims. A friend of mine knows of affluent, educated, "culturally Islamic" Syrians who have said exactly the same thing: It's the Jews' fault. They're pulling the strings from behind the curtains. Another belief common in the Muslim world is that the attack on the World Trade Center was a plot of Mossad, the Israeli intelligence agency, to turn the United States against the Arabs. Most recently, the former prime minister of Malaysia called for the Muslims of the world to unite against "Jewish global domination." At a speech in October 2003 he said the "Jews rule the world by proxy."

My conversation with my shopkeeper friend was a telling moment for me. I had been imagining that the

Christian Arabs might be able to provide a short-term solution to the current struggles between Israel and the Palestinians, if they would only say to the Muslims, "Enough of this! If you're not going to make peace with Israel, then *we'll* make peace with Israel."

But they'll never do that. It's as if their ethnicity transcends their religion. And if we are ever to be able to unravel the threads comprising the matrix of the Middle East, we need to understand how the different groups think. We need to understand the intricacies of the Middle Eastern mind, the differences and similarities between the various countries, the role of Islam, and the various divisions within Islam.

"You Send People to the Moon, But You Can't Even Fix Our Sewers."

That was an unidentified Iraqi's comment to an American on the challenges of rebuilding Iraq—fixing the infrastructure, bringing Western-style democracy to a country where 99 percent of the electorate voted for the same candidate (you can guess who) in his last election, and uniting religiously and ethnically disparate groups.

Perhaps—*perhaps*—it can be done. We know from the Bible it will be accomplished in the long term. But my experience in Iraq and the region in general has made me cautious about offering easy answers and simplistic solutions—and that's something Americans are all too eager to provide. We said, "All we have to do is get rid of Saddam Hussein, and we can bring democracy to

Iraq." Now that "we got him," the notion of a peaceful, democratic Iraq is a fragile one at best. We must make great care in trying to understand the dynamics between the Sunni and Shiite Muslims, a schism that dates back to the death of Muhammad in A.D. 632.

At Muhammad's death his followers split over who should lead the community. The Sunnis (whose name is from the Arabic word for *tradition*) supported those who had served in leadership under Muhammad. The Shiites (whose name is from the Arabic word for *follower*) believed the leadership should descend through Muhammad's bloodline. The resulting schism over leadership and succession produced two separate streams of Islam that, over the years, have developed significant theological and cultural differences. About 85 percent of all Muslims worldwide adhere to the Sunni branch of Islam, while the Shiites are a majority in countries like Iran and Iraq.

The average American knows that three great monotheistic religions originated in the Middle East—Judaism, Christianity, and Islam. And to our secular mind these are nothing more than three different "brands" of the same spiritual beverage—like choosing between Coke, Pepsi, and RC Cola.

But if the differences could be explained merely on the basis of "brand loyalty," then why is there such hatred and conflict on the part of Islam toward the other groups? Could there be something within their belief system itself that is the root cause for the ongoing strife? Why are the Muslims of the Middle East so opposed to the very existence of the State of Israel?

Why are they opposed to the presence of U.S. troops in Saudi Arabia or Kuwait or Afghanistan or Iraq? Can such hatred be explained on the basis of something other than the religious beliefs of Islam itself?

Is It Poverty?

After September 11, some in the media answered the prevalent question, "Why do Muslims hate America?" with the reply, "Because they're poor and we're not." It is true that most of the countries in the Middle East have more than their share of poverty. But if we look more closely, that explanation doesn't hold up. The hijackers who flew the jets into the Pentagon and the Twin Towers—and who crashed into the Pennsylvania countryside—were well educated and came from upper-middle-class Saudi and Egyptian families. Osama bin Laden came from a wealthy family that made its money in construction.

Trying to identify poverty as the root cause fails in other, similar conflicts. Certainly oil-rich Iraq and Iran did not go to war over economic issues. In their case, the enmity was at least partly due to ethnic differences, since Iranians are Persian and Iraqis are Arab. The Muslim guerillas in the southern Philippines are battling against the Christians in the north who seem to be equally impoverished. The bombing of the nightclub in Bali affected mostly tourists from Australia, and ultimately harmed the Muslims of Indonesia by delivering a body blow to their economy.

Poverty alone does not drive people to unceasing

conflict and implacable hostility. Nor are the problems primarily social in origin. Terrorists can be male or female, older or younger. We have to search elsewhere.

Is It Politics?

The political structures of the Middle East are quite diverse. Saudi Arabia is a monarchy but, like Iran, is also run as a theocratic state. Jordan is a constitutional monarchy, with emphasis on "monarchy." Iraq under Hussein was a relatively secular nation ruled by the Baath Party, as is Syria. Egypt is in theory a democracy, but it's also very corrupt. No commonality there—and yet all these countries have struggled with violence.

Is It Racial?

The truth is that the Jews and Arabs are more closely linked racially than, for example, the Afghans and the Saudis. Jews and Arabs certainly share more in common racially, historically, and linguistically than do Arabs and Indonesians. Yet most Arab nations have diplomatic relations with Indonesia, not Israel.

Having eliminated these causes, we now come to what is perhaps the central thread weaving the Middle East matrix.

Whose god is God?

Crusade.
What do you think of when you hear that word? A

Billy Graham gathering, perhaps, or a zealous reformer like Ralph Nader battling against corporate misdeeds. Or the failed efforts of medieval knights to retake the Holy Land for Christ. When President George Bush stood up after the September 11 attacks and announced that the United States would launch a "crusade" against those who had done this, that single word rang in Muslim ears with a clanging discordance. For most Americans, the word was nothing more than a metaphor for a determined fight.

But to Muslims, a *crusade* is a religious assault against Islam. Never mind that the First Crusade was launched in A.D. 1095, and that the age of the Crusades effectively ended in A.D. 1291, over seven hundred years ago! All they know is that Islam swept through the Middle East and overcame Christianity after the death of Muhammad. Centuries later, the infidels arrived in ships from the West on their holy Crusades to retake the land that now belonged to Allah. Ultimately, the crusaders failed, but they left a trail of Muslim blood in their wake. President Bush's one-time use of the word set off alarm bells throughout the Islamic world. They see our support for Israel as part of this crusade. They see Israel's control over Jerusalem and the Temple Mount—which they believe is the third holiest site in Islam—as an affront. They see the U.S. military presence in Afghanistan, Kuwait, and Iraq as an attempt to reoccupy the Holy Land for Christianity.

The Crusades remain a paradigm for understanding the relationship between Jews, Christians, and Muslims. Jews see the Crusades as a campaign by militant

Christianity against both Jews and Muslims. While the purpose for the Crusades was to liberate the Holy Land, Christians also used the occasion to promote attacks against the Jews of Europe and the Middle East. Christians often romanticize the Crusades as a time when knights in shining armor took to the field of battle to protect the honor of the Lord and of His church. Most Christians have little knowledge of the intrigue, treachery, and barbarity of the deeds committed against Jews in the name of Christ during that period.

Muslims see the Crusades as an attempt by the disobedient Christians—who were Islam's imperfect predecessors—to oppose Allah and thwart his plans for global conquest. They still view their relationships to modern-day Israel and to the "Christian West" through this same paradigm of conflict. To Muslims, the establishment of the State of Israel by the United Nations is but another attempt to retake land that rightfully belongs to Allah.

Muslims look back at a glorious, vanished past. Not everyone realizes that when Europe was mired in the Dark Ages, there was a great flowering of Islamic culture—including mathematics (*algebra* is from an Arabic word), astronomy, architecture, science, and medicine. Early medieval scholars traveled from Europe to the Arab world to be taught. Their buildings were beautiful; their decorative arts intricate; their societies well ordered. Even their hygiene was far superior. Part of what sparked the Renaissance was the influence of these Muslim scholars on southern Europe.

But then the two societies traded places. Gradually

the Arab and Islamic world drifted into the backwaters of global insignificance, while the "Christian West" ascended to its present political and cultural dominance. That rankles them: They were once great, and the infidel continues to conquer.

"Islamists . . . believe that once a country has been under Islamic rule it can never be relinquished," wrote Paul Marshall of the Center for Religious Freedom in the *Boston Globe*. "This is why Osama bin Laden insists he wants Spain back." (Much of Spain, of course, was under Muslim rule for several hundred years in the medieval era.)

To many Americans this type of reasoning can seem ludicrous. But it is how many Muslims think. And when we understand their matrix of reality, it sheds light on their seeming intransigence—and their willingness to blame the United States and Israel for many of the region's ills.

The Fractured Landscape

The Islamic world, however, is no more monolithic than the Christian world. Most Americans first heard about Shiite Muslims during the Iranian hostage crisis in 1979. The Ayatollah Khomeini, a Shiite religious leader, sought to establish a theocracy in Iran, which under the shah had been a secular monarchy with strong ties to the West. Other Islamic nations from the larger Sunni branch of Islam, such as Saudi Arabia, Kuwait, and Iraq (which has a majority Shiite population but which was ruled by Sunnis), became nervous over Iran exporting its brand of fundamentalism across their borders. Part of the reason Iraq went to war with Iran in 1980 was over these religious differences. Part of the reason was also ethnic. (The population of Iraq is largely Arab, while Iran is Persian.) And, to illustrate how fluid alliances can be in the region, the United States supported Iraq in its conflict with Iran.

Where does Osama bin Laden fit into this? He is described in the press as a Muslim fundamentalist, so it would be easy for us to assume that he shares much in common with the Muslim fundamentalists of Iran. But it would be wrong to make that assumption. Bin Laden subscribes to the Wahabi sect of Sunni Islam—a different branch of extreme Islamic fundamentalism that is prevalent in Saudi Arabia.

At the same time, most Muslims—be they Shiite or Sunni, Syrian or Saudi, Persian or Palestinian—would agree on one thing: Israel. It shouldn't be there. Muslims believe that land conquered for Allah belongs to Allah through all time. The fact that Israel now occupies land that should be under Islamic control is contrary to what the Quran teaches and is an offense to Allah. Now, too, the Crusaders are back, supporting Israel, controlling Afghanistan and Iraq, propping up the corrupt government in Saudi Arabia, and taking the oil that Allah gave to the Arabs. Islamic fundamentalists are convinced our ultimate goal is to take for ourselves the land that belongs to Allah.

We are perceived to be a threat to Islam—and that is why they fight; that is why they send suicide bombers over Manhattan. If the United States pulled completely out of the Middle East, if we dropped our support of Israel and let the land be overrun by Muslims, they would be happy. For now. But then Islamic fundamentalists would also control the oil that is the West's lifeblood, and that is not acceptable. So the conflict continues.

In the end, the question remains, "Whose god is God?"

Let Them Have It?

When we read such headlines as that seen in the *New York Times* recently, "No Illicit Arms Found in Iraq," we can't help but wonder, *Why are we there? Why do we keep rolling our tanks across their sand, and why do we keep meddling in their religion and their politics?* After all, we could use those billions of dollars here at home to rebuild our roads and shore up our schools.

The short answer to that question is: "September 11." And here our national case of short-term memory loss enters in. It is easy to forget the destruction of that day, easy to forget our sense of sudden vulnerability and violation. We used to think the terrorists were "out there"—but on September 11 the terrorists struck here, within our borders. They are gaining access to more and more weapons of mass destruction, and—for our own protection—we need to take the fight back to them.

The total cost to the United States for the attacks against the World Trade Center is still being calculated, and the amount will probably never be fully known. But a report entitled "Financial Impact of the World Trade

Center Attack" prepared for the New York State Senate Finance Committee provides a reasonable approximation. They estimate that the impact of the attack on the overall U.S. economy resulted in a decline in our nation's gross domestic product (GDP) of $745 billion from the fourth quarter of 2001 through the fourth quarter of 2003. This does not include the direct costs of the attack on the economy of New York, which they estimate to be somewhere between $32 and $51 billion in physical costs (rescue, recovery, and rebuilding) plus an additional $36–$54 billion in insurance payments.

The terrorists have attacked here. So we need to support the right of our government to pursue them there. But we also need to encourage our leaders to move ahead with great wisdom and sensitivity—so that the mistakes of the past are not repeated.

"A GENTLE ANSWER . . ."

I was in Baghdad in 1988. I had been invited there by the Iraqi government to attend the second Babylon Festival, showing off the rebuilding of the ancient city. I was eating dinner in my hotel when a man walked up—unannounced and uninvited—and sat down at my table. Barging in to eat with a solitary diner is out of character in any culture. I looked at him, and he simply said, "I need to talk with you."

He gave me his card, which identified him as an Iraqi press representative stationed at the United Nations. The reality was that he was probably one of their spies at the UN. And he asked, "Why do you Americans allow the Zionists to control you so much?"—the same question I was later asked by my Palestinian shopkeeper friend. This Iraqi "press official" launched into a discourse on "the peace-loving Iraqi people" and "the Zionist-controlled American press" that was seeking to turn the U.S. against his country. This was right after the U.S. had accused Iraq of using chemical weapons against the Kurds, and relations between the two countries were starting to sour.

His perspective, common in the Arab world, was that Israel was trying to drive a wedge between the U.S. and Iraq. I've heard variants of this story over and over: Israel had always been against Iraq. Israel destroyed the Osirak nuclear reactor in 1981. And when Saddam Hussein worked out another way to make Iraq a great nation, Israel took another tack and cooperated with the U.S. to sponsor the 1990 invasion of Iraq.

So I listened and didn't say much. The biblical verse that led me was, "A gentle answer turns away wrath, but a harsh word stirs up anger" (Proverbs 15:1). I just said to him, "That is very interesting. I've never heard that from your perspective. Thank you for sharing that with me." And that made him happy.

I first learned this lesson in Israel. I led a student group there, and we spent many hours in Jerusalem's Old City bargaining for souvenirs. One group of students went to a shop run by a merchant named Mufeed, whom we called "Murphy." They were bargaining, and just as they reached agreement on the price, another student came by and said, "Hey, I found that same thing for five bucks less in another shop!" Everyone followed him out of the shop, leaving Murphy alone . . . and without a sale.

That was one of the worst things they could have done in that culture, because the protocol is, once you've come to an agreement on price, you pay. Murphy followed the group back to where we were staying, and I met with him in the courtyard while the students were inside watching through the window. Murphy was shouting and gesturing wildly with his hands; the students were concerned that he might attack me. But I just kept saying, "You know, Murphy, you're right. That was very rude on their part, and they shouldn't have done that. I apologize to you on behalf of the group."

Murphy and I became great friends after that. I respected him, and I agreed that he was right. From an American's perspective, Arabs can appear to be overly emotional, sensitive, or passionate. But they also have a tremendous sense of what's right and what's wrong . . . and Americans could learn much from them about loyalty and friendship.

That was my first experience with what God taught me about "the gentle answer."

3
After the Statue Fell

"You, O king, were looking and behold, there was a single great statue; that statue, which was large and of extraordinary splendor, was standing in front of you, and its appearance was awesome."

Daniel 2:31

The toppling of the Saddam Hussein statue in Baghdad, a scene flashed around the world, joined the raising of the flag at Iwo Jima and the fall of the Berlin Wall as iconic images of triumph, victory, and conquest. Sadly, the celebrations in Baghdad were short-lived as it soon became obvious that the mere disappearance of Saddam, captured by coalition forces on December 14, 2003, hiding in a hole, was not enough to bring a divided nation to heel—let alone to turn on the lights or start the oil flowing. In the struggle since the war was declared "over" on May 1, 2003, more American soldiers have been killed than fell during the actual war itself, lending credence to the lament of one soldier's mother: "He's trying to bring freedom to them—but do they want it?"

Further complicating the picture is the increasingly divisive presence of some Shiite leaders thought to have ties to Iran and suspected of fomenting anti-American sentiment. The Shiite community is the largest population in Iraq, but under Hussein they were brutally oppressed: Sadr City, named after two Shiite clerics killed by Saddam Hussein in 1980 and 1999, is a slum section of Baghdad that is home to over two million Shiites. This has been a flashpoint of conflict and the location of frequent attacks on American patrols.

Plans call for the establishment of a new Iraqi government as quickly as possible. Even with Saddam Hussein now permanently out of the picture, the religious and economic instability in the country makes it hard to imagine an Iraq where democracy can flourish. Or, more significantly, how a government composed of so many diverse factions can rise above such factionalism to provide strong, unified leadership.

Still, there are intriguing links between what Scripture says and what we're reading and hearing about in news accounts. Let's try to trace some of them.

First, though, join me in Babylon.

"Saddam Hussein Invites You . . ."

I first became interested in that ancient city, whose name has become synonymous with hedonistic wealth and excess, when I was in college. I needed to write a paper for a theology class. I chose as my text Revelation

17–18, the passage that speaks of the fall of Babylon. Conventional wisdom among Bible scholars has held that, in that passage, "Babylon" was in fact a code word for Rome. I thought it would be an easy topic to research, so to the book of Revelation I went.

The problem was that as I actually started studying the passage, the Bible confounded my preconceptions. I wrote a fairly pathetic paper that said something like, "I know Babylon is supposed to be a symbolic representation of Rome, but the passage sure seems to have more in common with the Babylon of the Old Testament than it does to the city of Rome. But I know somehow it must be Rome." My professor, who was a master teacher, said, "Maybe you ought to pursue what the Bible says."

That got me thinking. Three years later, when I needed to write my seminary master's thesis, I again chose the identity of Babylon in Revelation 17–18 as my topic. As I worked on the thesis, I became more and more convinced that the Bible means what it says, and that the city referenced in Revelation is the *real* Babylon. Babylon, I discovered, is one key piece of the biblical puzzle that links the book of Revelation back to the book of Genesis. The Bible presents the city of Babylon in contrast to Jerusalem and God's program for the nation Israel. So that's how my love affair with Babylon began.

Later, my students would hear me "babble on about Babylon." One of them sent me notice of the first Babylon Festival to be held in Iraq in 1987. This was during the heart of the Iraq-Iran war, which had been going on for seven years and which Saddam was losing. But I wanted to go, so I wrote the Iraqi Embassy in Washington, D.C., informing them of my interest. Months passed and I finally received an invitation stating that my presence at the festivities was "vital."

In September I boarded a nighttime Lufthansa flight to Baghdad, sharing the plane with a group of German businessmen. When we arrived at the airport, I followed the Germans off the plane and found myself standing at the end of a long line of people waiting at Customs while their bags were checked. I walked up to a guard and said, "I'm here for this," holding up a little card I had been sent by the Iraqi embassy that had "Babylon Festival" and the name "Munir Bashir" on it. Apparently Mr. Bashir was a personage of some importance, for the guard ushered me to the front of the line and escorted me through, without opening my baggage. I was taken to the Ishtar Sheraton Hotel in downtown Baghdad, overlooking the square where the statue was later toppled. When I showed the clerk the magic card, I was given a room on the top floor next to the presidential suite.

The next day a group of us were shuttled by bus to Babylon, about an hour south of Baghdad. We were taken to the "Saddam Hussein guesthouse," where we found ourselves in a large room with tables where headphones were provided by language: English, French, German, and Arabic. A man stood up to welcome us and said, "I am Munir Bashir." The man whose name was on the card was Saddam Hussein's personal representative, running the Babylon Festival!

He said, "I'm pleased to have all of you world-famous ethnomusicologists here for this festival on ethnomusicology." I thought, *What? Why am I here?* I had all sorts of questions. But the verse that came to mind was from Proverbs: "Even a fool, when he keeps silent, is considered wise" (Proverbs 17:28). I had never consciously memorized that verse, but when I looked it up later, there it was. So I kept my mouth shut. We eventually got a brief tour of Babylon, but I wanted to see more of the city that had so captured my interest.

The next day the buses brought us back from Baghdad, but rather than following the group into the guesthouse again, I got off and walked about a quarter-mile back to where they were rebuilding Nebuchadnezzar's palace. Two journalists joined me for this impromptu tour. The only apparent obstacle blocking our way was a low wall (which is now a giant wall) around the palace perimeter. As we were getting ready to scale the wall, four Iraqi soldiers spotted us, called us over—and shared their lunch with us before waving good-bye to us as we climbed over the wall and into the city. We went into the great city and explored for about two hours. Was I afraid? No, because I had the sense that God wanted me there.

As I walked down the streets of ancient Babylon, two things went through my mind. One was the kid-in-a-candy-store sort of reaction: *Wow! I can't believe I'm here!* I had so studied the excavation reports on Babylon that I could find my way around with relative ease.

The other thought was inspired by the verses in Jeremiah and Revelation: "Flee from the midst of Babylon, and each of you save his life! Do not be destroyed in her punishment, for this is the LORD's time of vengeance; He is going to render recompense to her" (Jeremiah 51:6).

"Come out of her, my people, so that you will not partic-ipate in her sins and receive of her plagues" (Revelation 18:4). Get out, because God said a day is coming when the city would be destroyed forever. God's Word of warn-ing to anyone near that place was to flee because it's going to be destroyed. The echo of each footstep on the stone pavement seemed to alternate between whisper-ing "Wow!" and "Watch out!"

I came home from that trip thinking, *That was an incredible, once-in-a-lifetime experience.* Then I received a call from the Iraqi embassy that next spring, asking if I would like to go to the second Babylon Festival. "Oh, I'd love to," I said. "But I spent all my money going to the first." "Well, we'll pay your way," the official said.

That summer Iraq won its war with Iran. There were three major battles that devastated the Iranian army. Ayatollah Khomeini was forced to surrender even though, he said, it was a fate worse than "drinking a cup of poison." When I flew back to Iraq that Septem-ber, the whole atmosphere was different. The press was all excited; the people were friendly. They drove us to Tikrit, Saddam Hussein's hometown, and to Samarra, the site of an ancient mosque with its circular minaret that looks like a miniature Tower of Babel.

They even took us to see the weapons they had cap-tured from the Iranians during the final battles. The previous September, if you had walked up to someone in the street and spoken to him, his response would have been to look at you as if he were a deer staring into the headlights of an onrushing car. But in 1988 there was a brief period of euphoria and openness.

A Kinder, Gentler Hussein?

Now, of course, the city of Babylon sits in relative silence, as the Euphrates River flows by. Two small Iraqi villages still nestle within the ancient city limits, and a contingent of the multinational task force now occupies the buildings constructed by Saddam Hussein. The base is appropriately named Camp Babylon (see photo insert).

But my experience tells me a strong ruler will emerge out of the chaos of Iraq, perhaps a kinder, gentler version of Saddam Hussein—because it will take a Hussein-like strongman to hold that country together. Eventually, the oil will begin to flow. And these events will set the stage for the endgame.

It is in the best interests of the West to keep Iraq united, and Western governments will eventually embrace a strong leader in Iraq who can rein in all the competing factions. This leader will need to appeal to Iraq's rich history to bring about unity. He will need to get the people to see themselves as Iraqis once again, rather than Kurds, or Shiites, or Baathists. Like Saddam Hussein before him, he will discover the city of Babylon's symbolic power to unite and excite the masses. Construction will resume and Babylon will again move toward center stage in the love/hate relationship between the oil-rich Middle East and the oil-hungry West.

Here I must raise a caution. The Bible doesn't say exactly *when* these things will happen—only that they *will* happen. There will be twists and turns along the way; perhaps the Shiites could assume power. Perhaps the Kurds will make a concerted effort to break away and form their own country. But in the end a strong leader who is doing business with countries like Germany, France, and Russia will rebuild Iraq into an economic power. And this is exactly what the Bible predicts will take place.

We do not know how much time there is between now and then, but when we get to the "then," there will be two major forces in the world. There's an economic force pictured in the Bible as a woman who personifies evil. She is described as the city that gave birth to all the evil of the world, and she is named Babylon.

The second major force in the world is described in the Bible as a military powerhouse. Pictured symbolically as a "beast," this reconstituted Roman Empire will be a powerful European confederacy.

We see in the book of Revelation a new relationship between these two end-time powers. The kings of the world, the merchants of the world, and the sea captains of the world are all submitting to the military authority of this empire and its ruler. ("And they worshiped the beast, saying, 'Who is like the beast, and who is able to wage war with him?'" [Revelation 13:4].) At the same time they are also seeking to profit economically from their trade with the woman. ("For all the nations have drunk of the wine of the passion of her immorality, and the kings of the earth have committed acts of immorality with her, and the merchants of the earth have become rich by the wealth of her sensuality" [18:3].) Babylon becomes one of the driving economic forces in the West. They're selling things to her; they're transporting things to and from her; they're growing rich from her.

Iraq has the second-largest proven oil reserves in the world—and right now she has a very large shopping list. Eventually the economic situation will be resolved; and those companies that win Iraqi contracts for buildings, for roads, for the reconstruction of all other infrastructure, for supplying consumer goods, and for extracting and shipping oil will reap a tremendous bonanza. Such nations as Germany, France, and Russia want a say in who will participate in these deals. They were doing business with Iraq before the recent war and they're looking for those opportunities again, which helps in part to explain their opposition to U.S. policy in Iraq.

According to the Bible, a revived Roman Empire or new European confederacy will initially be in partnership with Babylon. We could be seeing the precursor to this confederacy in the establishment of the European Union. Certainly Europe actively sought out opportunities to trade with Saddam Hussein before the recent war. The "New Europe" would like to replace the U.S. as the dominant economic force in the Middle East.

Ultimately, that European confederacy will develop the symbiotic relationship with Iraq and Babylon pictured in the book of Revelation. But Europe will eventually tire of Babylon's economic bullying and will turn against this former ally. For that to happen Babylon must again rise as a great city. Note that Scripture doesn't say that Babylon has to be *built*, in the sense of having been completed. But it must be in existence and be identified as a place of influence and power. And it must control the economic resources of the Middle East in a way that allows it to have such influence on a resurging Europe.

When the Clock Starts Ticking

The clock will begin ticking on the unfolding of these events when the ruler of this new European confederacy makes a seven-year treaty with the nation of Israel (Daniel 9:27)—a treaty that will seem to ensure Israel's peace and safety. For three and a half years Israel will enjoy a state of relative peace. But then this ruler will enter the newly constructed temple and declare himself to be god, erect a statue of himself, and order the people to bow to the image. He will unleash his evil on God's people and will only be stopped when Christ returns at the end of the seven-year period.

In the meantime, this European leader will form an alliance of convenience with Babylon, wedding his military might with Babylon's economic power. But the ruler eventually grows tired of Babylon's economic oppression, possibly through its control of Middle East oil. Near the end of the seven years, when the time seems right, he attacks the city. The Bible tells us that Babylon will be destroyed by an army converging on her "from a far country" (Isaiah 13:5).

Writing a hundred years later, Jeremiah adds that these forces will sweep down from the north (50:9). Isaiah also identifies the "Medes" as part of the armies (13:17). The Medes were a people who lived in the mountainous areas of northeastern Iraq and northwestern Iran—the same region now occupied by the Kurds, who cooperated with the U.S. in the war against Iraq in 2003. The Kurds, you may recall, experienced the reality of Saddam Hussein's weapons of mass destruction in 1987 and 1988 when he used chemical weapons to slaughter thousands of Kurdish civilians. It is not difficult to make the connection between them and their ancient ancestors, the Medes.

But, you might ask, how can Babylon rise economically from pauper to princess in such a short time? Iraq today is an economic basket case with crumbling infrastructure, a shattered economy, political instability, and a crushing debt load from twenty-five years of despotic rule under the harsh hand of Saddam Hussein. Isn't the idea of a rags-to-riches rise for Babylon a little far-fetched?

Two keys help unlock this mystery. The first is the key of *history*. Several historical parallels can help us understand how Babylon's rapid rise could come about. At the end of World War II much of Europe was a shattered ruin. The Marshall Plan helped bring about a relatively rapid recovery. At the same time the island empire of Japan also lay in ruins, but it also recovered with the help of outside assistance—specifically from the decade-long American occupation. Today the United States is seeking to raise billions of dollars from nations around the world to help rebuild Iraq. The recovery could be dramatic.

The second key is the economic impact of oil. Iraq sits on the second-largest proven oil reserves in the world. As the world's economy again begins to expand, the demand for oil will grow. Iraq's ability to supply large quantities of oil will generate sufficient capital to sustain the nation's growth.

Babylon will rise again—only to fall one last time. John's vision in Revelation 17–18 vividly tells of Babylon's destruction, of the weeping of the merchants and the rejoicing in heaven. She will burn, and her wealth will be only ashes.

But Jerusalem—ah, that is another story.

"THIS IS NOT THE RIGHT ROAD"

I'm often asked if I'm ever afraid when I go to the Middle East. Usually, I'm not—of course, you have to know where to go and where not to go.

But there was one time . . .

I have a dear friend who drives tour buses in Israel. He's an unusual combination: an Arab Christian, born in Nazareth, and an Israeli citizen. He is also a careful, skilled driver and a gentle, kind individual who becomes a dear friend to all the travelers in the group. He now drives for all the tours I guide.

The first time I ever had him as a bus driver, though, we got lost. You see, he had driven mostly for "touristy tours," whereas I like to take people to some sites that are off the beaten path. On this particular day we were leaving a place called Nebi Samwil, which could be the ancient biblical site of Mizpah. I wanted to go down one specific road, but suddenly Munir was turning left. "Oh, Munir, I thought we would go this way," I said.

"No, this is a shortcut," he replied. At least he thought it was a shortcut.

He turned and in a few minutes we were driving into a village called Bidu. Bidu is a Palestinian town, and hasn't always been peaceful. If a car with Israeli license plates stumbled into Bidu, the driver ran the risk of getting a rock thrown through his or her windshield. Bidu is not a place to take tourists!

The problem was that there was no way the bus could slip through the village unobserved. We had to negotiate a sharp right-hand turn in the middle of the village. I was sitting up front and Munir said quietly, "This is not the right road."

"Don't tell anybody," I said, thinking of our fellow passengers behind us. We went around the corner and the townspeople were staring at us, too shocked at seeing a tour bus driving through their dusty village to throw stones. We left the village, and as we drove up a hill, Munir and I both felt a sense of relief. Suddenly, as the bus topped the hill we saw a large group of Arab laborers walking toward us, carrying sickles, rakes, and pitchforks. It looked like a mob approaching the bus.

Munir opened his side window and, while still driving, began shouting in Arabic, "We are your friends. We are just Americans. I am an Arab and I'm coming through your area." Then he whispered to me in English, "Just wave," as he resumed shouting out the window in Arabic, "We are your friends."

Everyone on the bus was thinking, *Oh, how neat! The villagers are coming to see us!* They all started waving and smiling—and the crowd parted and let us through.

Now whenever I drive with Munir, I'll turn to him and say, "Bidu," and he'll laugh. But it certainly wasn't funny at the time. That was the only time in all my travels that I was really scared, because we were in a place we shouldn't have been.

But it was funny. (Though my wife, who wasn't on the trip, adds, "It might be funny now . . . but you didn't think it was funny then!")

In the Middle East, Jihadists were always known to chant, "Today's Saturday and tomorrow's Sunday" (*al-yom al sabt wa ghadan al-ahad*), alluding to their war against the Jews first, then followed by the Christians. [But now] for the soldiers of bin Laden around the world there is only one day from now on: Saturday is Sunday. Hopefully moderate Muslims will hasten the long-awaited reform, without which holy wars will continue to engulf civilization.

—**Walid Phares,** professor of Middle East studies and a terrorism expert (townhall.com, 10/09/03)

4

The Land, the People, the Puzzle

The first to plead his case seems just, until another comes and examines him.

Proverbs 18:17

Sadly, my friend Munir has not worked steadily in about three years.

I traveled to Israel twice in 2003, once in March and once in June, and Munir was the driver for both groups. But during the three-month period between those two trips his bus sat empty, another casualty of the conflict between Israel and the Palestinians that has devastated the tourism industry. And Munir is one of the more popular drivers, an open, friendly man who speaks fluent Arabic, Hebrew, and English.

He is not alone in his plight. We hear a lot about death tolls from various attacks, but little about the other human cost. Tourism is Israel's number one industry, employing thousands, but the constant strife has sent tourism plummeting. Hotels that used to employ hundreds of Arab workers are down to hiring a handful on a part-time, as-needed basis. When I took a group to Jerusalem in June 2003, there were twelve of us—and we were the largest group staying at the Hyatt hotel. There was only one other group staying at the hotel, and it was a group of ten from the United States. That was it.

The hotel gave us incredible service, and the workers—both Jewish and Arab—came up and thanked us just for being there. But if you look more closely at virtually all the hotels in Israel, they look tired and run down. Decorative exterior lights still shine, but often only half the lightbulbs are lit because, it seems, there is no one to replace them if they burn out. Many hotels have closed their main dining rooms and are serving the few guests they have in the coffee shops. And all those empty rooms and silent banquet halls represent thousands of people without jobs—both Jewish and Arab. According to the Poverty Report, released by Israel's National Insurance Institute in October 2003, 21 percent of all Israelis live under the poverty line. And one of every three children is impoverished.

But if the cost of the current conflict to Israelis is high, among Palestinians it is horrific. According to the charity Christian Aid, three-quarters of the Palestinian population in the West Bank and Gaza Strip are living on less than two dollars a day. Nearly 60 percent of all Palestinians now live under the poverty line, and the unemployment rate in the West Bank and Gaza Strip stands at 45 percent.

That's part of the human cost. But the crisis has also brought a high cost to human dignity. It's humiliating for Palestinians to have to go through the Israeli checkpoints, humiliating for a Muslim woman who is covered from head to toe to be frisked in public, even if it is a woman soldier doing the frisking.

But what are the Israelis to do when Palestinian men and women are crossing into Jewish areas and blowing themselves—and others—up? How can a society *not* respond when innocent women and children are torn to shreds by bombs packed with nails? The checkpoints are necessary because of the suicide bombers who actively seek out innocent civilians as targets. And Israelis are also subjected to searches of their purses, shopping bags, and backpacks every time they walk into a mall, store, or restaurant. As someone with friends on both sides of the conflict, I can see valid grievances on both sides, and I can certainly sorrow over the human suffering and pray for the innocent victims on both sides.

A Proper Diagnosis

Many of us wonder if there's any, *any* long-term, once-and-for-all answer to the Israeli-Palestinian question. As we have seen, the very existence of Israel lies at the heart of the Islamic world's antipathy toward the West and toward the U.S. in particular. It's related to the situation in Iraq; it's related to September 11 and the war on terror. All of these threads come together to form an intricate, complex pattern. But it is a pattern that we must seek to understand because we ignore it at our own peril.

Why, when agreements are reached, does the precarious peace always seem to fall apart? Well, imagine going to the doctor with an illness. You know you're pretty sick, but you're not sure what it is. The doctor diagnoses you with strep throat and prescribes antibiotics and rest. But in actuality, you have cancer. The doctor overlooked a few key symptoms that would have led to the correct diagnosis. Her failure to spot all the necessary clues caused the misdiagnosis. The result is that the treatment prescribed by the doctor is ineffective, and you get sicker.

That's the same thing that has happened in our attempt to diagnose and treat the conflict between Israel and the Palestinians. All the negotiations over territory and specific borders miss the fundamental issue causing the tension and strife—Islam's religious struggle with Judaism and Christianity. The reason the Camp David Accords, brokered by Jimmy Carter in 1978 with Menachem Begin of Israel and Anwar Sadat of Egypt, were effective was, in part, because the land in dispute (the Sinai peninsula) did not have religious significance. Israel gave back land that the Bible, in Numbers 34 and Ezekiel 47, did not include within her divine boundries. And Egypt chose to defer all issues related to the final status of Jerusalem. Had the issue of Jerusalem been pressed, the talks would have collapsed because no common ground for compromise was possible.

Israel's primary argument for possessing the land is religious. They would say, "This is the land God promised to the descendants of Abraham, Isaac, and Jacob, and we are the people to whom God has given it. He has outlined specific land boundaries, and He has told us that this land is ours."

The Muslims counter with their own religious argument. "You have been dispossessed as a people. God was so angry with you that He replaced you with the Christian church, and Christianity, in turn, was replaced by Islam. You have no rights to this land; it belongs to Allah. Not so much as one acre of this land can be controlled by an independent, sovereign nation of Israel. You may live in the land as Jews, but you cannot control it. We cannot grant you sovereignty over it, because it isn't ours to give. It belongs to Allah."

This helps explain why Anwar Sadat was assassinated in 1981 after becoming the first major Muslim head of state to recognize publicly Israel's right to exist as a nation. When he signed the peace treaty between Egypt and Israel, acknowledging Israel's right to control the land, he was acting against the revealed will of Allah. Members of the Muslim Brotherhood (a fundamentalist Muslim group with ties to al-Qaeda) targeted him for death for what they saw as a blasphemous act.

No matter how hard we try to rid the world of terrorists, the underlying problem still remains. And that problem is the deep, fundamental religious philosophy that says, "Everything once conquered for Allah belongs to Allah." The very existence of the State of Israel challenges the authoritative claims of Islam.

So Is There a Solution?

In one sense Palestinians do have a legitimate claim to at least part of the land. Some families who were driven off their land in 1948 and 1967 had lived there for centuries. And the Bible commands Israel to treat with fairness and dignity those non-Israelis who live in their midst. As Israel prepared to enter the land for the very first time, God made His will on this matter very clear. "You shall not wrong a stranger or oppress him, for you were strangers in the land of Egypt" (Exodus 22:21).

In the book of Ezekiel, written during the time when Israel was in captivity in Babylon, the prophet looked forward to a day when Israel would again return to her land. But even as God announced the ultimate fulfillment of His promises to Israel, He made it clear that Israel's blessing could not come at the expense of others. "It will come about that you shall divide [the land] by lot for an inheritance among yourselves and among the aliens who stay in your midst, who bring forth sons in your midst. And they shall be to you as the native-born among the sons of Israel; they shall be allotted an inheritance with you among the tribes of Israel" (Ezekiel 47:22).

So we're faced with the seemingly irresolvable tension between two opposing positions. Is there a way out of this dilemma? The ultimate biblical solution is to distinguish between individual rights of ownership and the overarching issue of national sovereignty. God expects the Jewish people to respect the individual ownership rights of all who live in the land, including those who are not Jewish. But God granted national sovereignty of the land to the Jewish people.

Let me give an example to help illustrate the difference between individual rights of ownership and national sovereignty. I own my home. (Actually, my wife and I are still paying off our mortgage, but we are the legal owners of the property.) I have individual rights of ownership. I can landscape the yard, change the carpet, or paint the walls any color I want. But I don't have sovereignty over my land. I cannot install a tollbooth on my sidewalk and charge people for using it. I cannot declare my independence and cease to pay state or county property taxes. And the state has the right to exercise its power of eminent domain to take my property from me should that serve the greater public good (to expand a highway or build a park, for example). They are expected to provide fair compensation if they seize my property, but my individual rights of ownership do not supersede their governmental sovereignty.

It was Ehud Barak, one of Israel's recent prime ministers, who described the current situation between Israel and the Palestinians as a "painful divorce." And, like many couples going through such a divorce, one of the first steps toward resolution needs to be physical separation between the two antagonists. In one sense this is what the Israelis are attempting to do by building a fence to separate Israelis and Palestinians. That's never a long-term solution (as the Chinese found out centuries ago), but the goal is to protect Israel in the short term. The major concern is that such a fence, once built, will establish a permanent border between Israel and the Palestinians. And, from the Palestinian perspective, the fence is being erected on their side of the property line—creating a border that permanently encroaches on land that belongs to them.

Another stumbling block to peace is Islamic fundamentalism, especially the activity of groups like Hamas
and Islamic Jihad. Every time the Israelis and Palestinians seem to get close to reaching an agreement, the
instances of terror jump dramatically. Hamas and Islamic
Jihad claim responsibility for most of these attacks—
which are launched to derail any peace treaty. Until the
Palestinian leadership dismantles the terrorist infastruc-
ture, the situation won't change.

What restrains Israel, with her military might, from
simply wiping out her enemies? First and foremost, we—
the U.S.—do. Even now, as Israel is building this fence,
the United States is saying, "If the specific route of the
fence inflames the situation, we're going to reduce our financial aid or take away our loan guarantees." And because
Israel needs our assistance—financially and militarily—they do listen when the U.S. government speaks.

Europe, which is Israel's major trading partner, also
has significant influence over her. It's true that anti-
Semitism is on the upswing in Europe; it's also true that
Europe's Muslim population is burgeoning. But Israel
and Europe have historic ethnic and cultural ties, and
Europe acts as a restraining influence.

Israel, of course, was founded by Ashkenazi—that
is, European—Jews, the vast majority of whom came from
a more liberal, tolerant tradition. They were impacted by
the bigotry and religious intolerance of the Russian czars
and Hitler's Nazi Party. For years they dominated Israeli
political and cultural life and acted as a brake on Israeli
response to Arab hostility. They tend to be more secular,
and they tend to be strong advocates for individual reli-

gious and civil rights. Recently a group of Israeli Air Force pilots signed a public declaration stating, "We think it's wrong to bomb Palestinian population centers in these targeted attacks." I suspect that if you tracked them down, you'd discover the vast majority were Ashkenazi Jews.

On the other side are the Sephardic Jews who have come to Israel from Muslim nations. This group has emerged as a major force in Israel's political landscape. They are more aggressive and less tolerant than the Ashkenazim—partly because they've seen what it's like to be a persecuted minority in an Arab-run society. And they're saying, "We're not going to let that happen again." The Sephardic Jews have a higher birthrate than the Ashkenazim. A demographic clock is ticking that will eventually push Israel toward a more aggressive stance.

Israel and the Bomb

Israel's most widely known state secret is that the country possesses several hundred nuclear weapons. Books like *The Sampson Option* by Seymour Hersh (Random House, 1991) and *Israel and the Bomb* by Avner Cohen (Columbia, 1998) document the development of Israel's nuclear program. The Arab nations know that Israel possesses nuclear weapons. They also know that in any face-to-face military confrontation with Israel—even if Israel only used its conventional weapons—they would lose.

But should they ever truly threaten Israel militarily, Israel has the ability to deliver a devastating nuclear strike against every major Muslim nation in the Middle

East. That is why many Muslim countries are seeking to develop their own nuclear, biological, and chemical weapons—nonconventional weapons of mass destruction—and seeking to obtain missile systems capable of launching these weapons into Israel's heartland.

During the most recent war with Iraq we sent Special Ops troops into western Iraq looking for Scud missile launchers, which could carry chemical or biological weapons to attack Israel. Because of the Holocaust, in which millions of Jews died from being gassed with Zyklon B, Israel will not tolerate any attack with chemical or biological weapons. If Hussein had launched such weapons against Israel, she would have retaliated with a nuclear strike.

The 1991 Gulf War, when Saddam lobbed Scuds at Israel, was the first time Israel did not respond when attacked. Up until that point, whenever the PLO or surrounding Arab countries struck at Israel, she would strike back. But during the Gulf War President Bush phoned the Israeli leaders urging them not to retaliate. To this day, there's a debate in Israel that her nonresponse during the first Gulf War was a mistake; that it projected weakness, not strength, and sent the wrong message.

Israel's conventional military strength might be unassailable now, but its vulnerability during the 1973 Yom Kippur War is another story. The Arab armies of Egypt and Syria launched an attack against Israel that caught the Jewish nation by surprise. The initial American response to Israel's pleas for help was to do nothing. "Go through the UN," we told her. "Work through the proper channels." But the military equipment we had supplied Israel was being chewed up at an alarming rate by the onslaught on the Golan Heights and in the Sinai. As the Arab armies pressed their attack, Israel's military situation grew ever more precarious. According to Seymour Hersh, it was during the dark days of the Yom Kippur War that Israel went on full nuclear alert for the first time in their history. Syria was threatening to overrun the Golan Heights and capture all of Galilee. Had that happened, Israel was prepared to use its nuclear weapons against the Syrian troops.

When it became apparent to the United States that our refusal to resupply Israel with conventional weapons could force them to use their nuclear arsenal, we opened our armament spigot and began an emergency airlift to Israel. We actually depleted our supply of weapons in Western Europe to ship tanks and other equipment to Israel—and we did this at a time when we were on full Cold War readiness, on alert for a Soviet attack across the border between East and West. Then we had to resupply our European forces quickly, lest we leave ourselves vulnerable for too long. But at that point in time the danger of events in the Middle East sparking a nuclear conflagration were far more serious of a threat to world peace than any potential Soviet aggression in Europe.

At the present time, if Israel were to be attacked by her neighbors again and truly threatened, the United States would step in and supply whatever equipment she needed. It is less clear whether we would place our troops in harm's way, but we would send equipment—and one primary reason is that if Israel were left without the means to fight a conventional war, she would be forced to turn to unconventional warfare. And that, to the United States, is unacceptable.

A "Peace Partner"?

Meanwhile, many Israelis, especially those in the more liberal wing, are coming to the conclusion that an outside agent needs to step in and mediate the current Middle East conflict. While the United States has been the primary outside agent seeking to bring peace to the Middle East, there are some who believe the need exists for a new set of peace partners. The current hopes rest on the efforts of the "quartet" composed of the United States, the European Union, Russia, and the United Nations. The goal is to have these four outside powers team up to broker a peace plan. This plan would include several stages, and the implementation of the agreement would, according to former Israeli Prime Minister Shimon Peres, take "a number of additional years." The new "road map to peace" was proposed in 2002. Unfortunately, we all know the fate of that road map, at least so far.

This new road map to peace did teach us three things about what will be needed to bring about peace in the Middle East. First, peace will require an outside partner or partners. The Israelis and Palestinians do not trust one another. An "honest, outside broker" is needed to help negotiate—and implement—any agreement. Second, peace will take time, more rather than less. So many deadlines and timetables have come and gone that those opposed to peace believe they can simply wait out any agreement. It will take time to build trust and navigate through the incremental steps along the way. Third, a strong military presence is essential to enforce any agreement. No peace will succeed unless something can be done to eliminate the threat of terrorism.

Now consider: What if someone were to come along and say, "Here's the agreement; here's how it's going to work out. I'll help enforce it, and it's going to take seven years to implement"?

This is where we have to turn from the morning paper and the cable news channels to our Bibles for a look at another sort of peace plan for Israel.

OTHER VIEWS

Christian Pilgrims' Support Helps
Israel "Keep on Going"

The thousands of Christians who have arrived this week to celebrate the biblical holiday of Succoth are boosting the morale of Israelis, who are standing on the front lines in the war against terrorism, Israeli Prime Minister Ariel Sharon's spokesman said.

For the fourth year in a row, Christians from around the world have braved the threat of terrorism and dismal security reports to show up by the thousands for the International Christian Embassy Jerusalem (ICEJ)'s Feast of Tabernacles Celebration.

The ICEJ is a Christian Zionist organization that supports the biblical teaching that the land of Israel, including the West Bank, known biblically as Judea and Samaria, as well as the Gaza Strip, are part of the eternal inheritance of the Jewish people and that Jerusalem is the capital of the Jewish people.

As such, the ICEJ is at the forefront of worldwide Christian support for the State of Israel. . . .

Sharon greeted this year's participants, who packed Jerusalem's largest convention center, welcoming the opening night crowd to Jerusalem, "the capital of the Jewish people" and the "united and undivided capital of the state of Israel forever. . . .

"For the past three years, we have been facing a war that was imposed upon us by the Palestinians. But the war did not start three years ago. It is a struggle that started over 120 years ago," Sharon said.

"Its root causes are the refusal of the Arab world to accept and reconcile with the birthright of the Jewish people to a democratic Jewish state in our ancestral homeland, in the cradle of the Jewish people. . . ."

On her 14th trip to Israel since 1995, Laurie Chalifoux, 54, a mother of two and grandmother of four, said her family was . . . comfortable about her taking a trip to Israel now.

"I came to show my support for Israel and to love the Jewish people," Chalifoux said. "The Bible gives us the admonition to 'comfort, comfort, my [God's] people,' and that's why I came; not only the Jews, but the Arabs as well."

—From a report by **Julie Stahl,** Jerusalem Bureau Chief, CNSNews.com, Crosswalk.com, 10/13/03

5
Israel: Right or Wrong?

"And I will bless those who bless you, and the one
who curses you I will curse. And in you all the
families of the earth shall be blessed."

Genesis 12:3

"The Lord your God will inflict all these curses on
your enemies and on those who hate you, who
persecuted you."

Deuteronomy 30:7

Just like the pilgrims in the preceding story,
most evangelical Christians in America strongly support Israel—seventy million, according to some surveys.
Yet this support is not unanimous. Some American Christians point to believing Arab brothers and sisters in the
Middle East and ask, "What about them?" Others wonder whether God's promises extend to the modern-day
State of Israel, a diverse nation whose people range from
intensely devout to avowedly secular. Has Israel main-
tained her covenant with God?

Part of the problem is that Israel doesn't easily con-
form to whatever stereotype evangelical Christians want

to give it. Three prominent, but incorrect, stereotypes exist among American evangelicals. First, some view Israel as the land of the rural kibbutz pioneers, whose members caused the desert to bloom during the day and defended their land against bands of marauding Arabs at night. While many of the early pioneers did join in the kibbutz movement, today less than 2 percent of all Israelis live on a kibbutz. Over 90 percent of the Jewish population of Israel live in urban, not rural, areas. Israel is not a quaint, rural land; it is a modern, developed nation.

Second, some view Israel as the land of the deeply pious sage, epitomized in the bearded Hasidim praying fervently at the Western Wall. But the ultra-Orthodox Jews comprise less than 30 percent of the population of Jerusalem, Israel's holiest city. And they make up only 10 percent of the total population of all Israel. Over 70 percent of the Jewish population of Israel characterize themselves as secular or nonreligious Jews.

Third, some view Israel less charitably as the land of militaristic, oppressive tyrants, led by a prime minister who is responsible for the deaths of hundreds of Palestinians. But the reality is that most of the charges made against Israel and its leaders—when examined carefully—have been shown to be false. Ariel Sharon was cleared of direct involvement in the attacks by Christian militiamen on the Sabra and Shatila refugee camps near Beirut, Lebanon, in 1982. That event had its roots in the conflict between Lebanon's Muslim and Christian communities. Likewise the charges of an Israeli massacre in the Jenin refugee camp in April 2002 were subsequently proven to be false. Unfortunately, the press often reports the initial charges as the lead story on the evening news while the report from the subsequent investigation receives scant attention. By the time the full report is released it has become "old news."

America's condemnation of Israel for her actions against the Palestinians' uprising has been more muted since September 11, 2001. Perhaps this is because we now understand, in part, the difficult choices they have had to make for over fifty-five years—and it makes us more sympathetic and understanding. We must deplore the loss of all innocent life, but we must also realize that terrorists often use civilians as human shields in their cowardly attacks against other civilians. There are no easy choices when fighting this type of war.

But returning to the original issue, should evangelical Christians support Israel's right to exist as a nation because of her special relationship to God? Some Christians, most notably pastor and author John Piper in a much-discussed article in *World* magazine on May 11, 2002, say no. Piper says that a "non-covenant-keeping people" have no right to the land and points to Leviticus 26 and Deuteronomy 28 to bolster his argument.

Leviticus 26 lists the good things that will come to the Israelites if they follow the Lord's commands—and the misfortunes that will befall them if they don't. "I will appoint over you a sudden terror, consumption and fever that shall waste away the eyes and cause the soul to pine away," God warns. "I will scatter [you] among the nations and will draw out a sword after you, as your land becomes desolate and your cities become waste" (vv. 16, 33).

Deuteronomy 28 paints an even bleaker picture, enumerating the curses that will come upon Israel if she is disobedient: diseases, drought, and destruction. "If you are not careful to observe all the words of this law which are written in this book," God warns, ". . . you shall be torn from the land where you are entering to possess it" (vv. 58, 63).

God's Yardstick—and Ours

God unquestionably holds Israel accountable for obedience to His covenant. And part of this accountability does now center on the issue of accepting Jesus as their Messiah. But how God regulates His blessings and cursings is between Him and the Jewish people. God also has provided standards by which He regulates His treatment of Gentiles. So the question for non-Jews becomes, what does He hold *us* accountable for?

Clearly, in Scripture, God holds non-Jews accountable for their treatment of Israel—apart from Israel's spiritual condition. In Genesis 12, Abram disobeyed God in leaving the land and traveling to Egypt, and he also tried to deceive Pharaoh by pretending that his wife, Sarai, was his sister. But when Pharaoh took Sarai as one of his concubines, God brought on Pharaoh and his household serious diseases (v. 17). Even though Pharaoh didn't initially know of Abram's deception, he suffered because of his treatment of Abram; God wanted to protect the mother of Israel and preserve His plan of redemption through Abram.

Even in the "cursing" passages in Deuteronomy 28

(cited above) God promises that He will not forget Israel and that He will still hold Gentiles accountable for their treatment of His people. In Deuteronomy 30 God announces that He will restore Israel to the land when they repent, and He also promises to punish the nations that had mistreated the Jews when they were under God's judgment. "The Lord your God will inflict all these curses on your enemies and on those who hate you, who persecuted you" (30:7). In the tiny book of Obadiah God succinctly summarizes His rule for evaluating nations. "As you have done [to Israel], it will be done to you" (Obadiah 15). There will be a "day of the Lord" when God will judge the nations, and He says that as the nations have treated Israel, so will they be treated in kind by Him.

Israel's conditional possession of the land, based on obedience, is between her and God. It's God who can sovereignly choose to remove her from the land; it's God who puts her back in the land. And since Israel is in the land right now, God must have a purpose for them being there, even if they are not there in obedience.

But God promised Abraham that He would bless those who blessed him and curse those who cursed him. Our job, therefore, is to make sure we're a blessing to the Jewish people. Biblically speaking, then, we do need to support Israel's right to exist as a nation.

What About the Arabs?

It's important, however, that Christians make it clear that we don't necessarily approve of everything the Israeli government does, *and* that we do not hate Arabs.

There have been some evangelicals who are so strong and vocal in their support for Israel that they have communicated a sense of hostility toward Arabs. It troubles me deeply when I hear an evangelical say the solution to the Middle East crisis is to force the Arabs out of the land and give it all to Israel.

In reality, the Bible makes it clear that even in God's ideal future plan for Israel He permits foreigners to live in the land. As noted in the previous chapter, God told Israel that when He ultimately restores Israel to her land, "'You shall divide it by lot for an inheritance among yourselves and among the aliens who stay in your midst, who bring forth sons in your midst. And they shall be to you as the native-born among the sons of Israel; they shall be allotted an inheritance with you among the tribes of Israel. And it will come about that in the tribe with which the alien stays, there you shall give him his inheritance,' declares the Lord God" (Ezekiel 47:22–23).

That isn't a passage we hear very much. But throughout the Old Testament God tells His people they will be judged on how they treat the aliens and strangers in their midst. So simply to imply that the solution is to expel the Palestinians is wrong.

Moreover, not all American Christians realize that there are many Arab believers who are caught between the Jews and the Muslims. Many Israelis don't understand or appreciate the differences between a Palestinian Christian and a Palestinian Muslim, so if you're a Palestinian you experience prejudice that supersedes being a Christian. The Palestinian Christians also suffer from the Muslim side because Muslims look down on Christians, even though they're the same ethnicity. Palestinian Christians are caught in the crossfire, and we need to be praying for them.

Jesus the Messiah

Jewish believers—one of whom I'll introduce you to—also struggle. Evangelicals who blindly support Israel don't realize that the ultra-Orthodox Jews in Israel are today's Pharisees, and they persecute believers in Jesus as vehemently as they did during the time of the apostle Paul. To be a Jewish follower of Jesus is to have a tough existence in Israel. While an Israeli citizen cannot lose his or her citizenship by becoming a follower of Jesus, the privilege of Israeli citizenship is denied to Jews seeking it if they do profess faith in Him. If you had been born and raised Jewish, if your parents were Jews and your grandparents were Jews *and* you accepted Jesus as your Messiah, you cannot claim your citizenship as an Israeli, even though by law every Jew has the right of return and should be able to claim Israeli citizenship.

If you say, "I am a Jew who practices Hinduism and I want to immigrate to Israel," or "I am a Jew who practices Buddhism and I want to come to Israel," that's fine. But you cannot legally immigrate to Israel and become a citizen if you claim Jesus as your Messiah.

Yet God is beginning to do great things in Israel. Eric and Terri Morey live in Galilee and run a business called The Galilee Experience that features a video history of the Galilee region, which includes a short segment on the life of Jesus. Though the entire program is very pro-Israel—and the segment on the life of Jesus is presented with great sensitivity—they had to fight all the way to Israel's Supreme Court for permission to show it. But they did receive permission. On one occasion an Orthodox Jew threw a Molotov cocktail at the screen during a performance in an attempt to destroy the entire theater. But the fire was put out and the theater was spared.

What is it about the video that stirs such passionate hatred? It is the short segment that focuses on Jesus of Galilee. It portrays Jesus as a Jew (something many Jews do not realize) and presents His claims in an irenic spirit. The presentation provides an opportunity for Israelis to learn about Jesus in a nonthreatening way. But even that is too much for some to tolerate. And that's just one example.

By some estimates there are at least six thousand Israelis who have professed belief in Jesus as their Messiah, and more than one hundred Messianic congregations are scattered throughout the country, many of which have formed within the last fifteen years. God is moving!

Still, both Jewish and Arab believers live with tensions we cannot begin to imagine. We can sit in the relative safety of our homes and communities and try to understand the situation intellectually. But what does "love your enemies" mean when you're watching friends get shot or relatives get blown up on buses? What does "turn the other cheek" mean when those on the other side want your wife and children dead?

Praying for "the Peace of Jerusalem"

Sunday after Sunday, in churches throughout our nation, Christians are reminded to "pray for the peace of Jerusalem" (Psalm 122:6). As followers of Christ who feel a pull toward the land of Abraham, David, and Jesus Himself, we mourn over the continuing violence and hatred—yet, after so many years of strife, we're no longer sure how to pray. It can seem so futile. But God has commanded it. How then should we pray?

Within Psalm 122 King David himself provides at least a partial answer. Jerusalem was significant because of God's *presence* ("Let us go to the house of the Lord," v. 1) and God's *purpose* ("For there thrones were set for judgment, the thrones of the house of David," v. 5). Peace provided the Israelite pilgrims with personal safety as they traveled to Jerusalem to worship their God. Peace was also the by-product of a righteous king sitting on the royal throne. So how does David's command to pray for the peace of Jerusalem affect our actions today?

Short-term, we need to be praying that God would give leaders—in the United States and in Israel—wisdom to thwart the attempts of evil men to harm innocent lives. As I was writing this book, I heard a report on the evening news that Osama bin Laden issued yet another new tape threatening further terrorist actions, and the FBI believes the tape is authentic. In our wired age, al-Qaeda and their affiliates are recruiting would-be terrorists over the Web. We cannot grow complacent; we cannot let our attention drift. The terrorists are plotting acts of destruction throughout the world—

including Iraq, Israel, and the United States—and they have no intention of stopping. But God has given us permission to seek His help in thwarting these activities. We should pray specifically that the plots come to light, that the government hears about them, and that the offenders are found and brought to justice.

Remember, too, Paul's instructions that we make "entreaties and prayers, petitions and thanksgivings . . . for kings and all who are in authority, so that we may lead a tranquil and quiet life in all godliness and dignity" (1 Timothy 2:1–2). We often pray for the president; but we should also remember those on the front lines in the various Middle Eastern countries—from the civilian authorities trying to bring order in Iraq, to those working toward a resolution of the Israeli-Palestinian question, to the soldiers who are seeking to maintain the peace.

We need to inform ourselves beyond the headlines and predictable television images so that we can pray with knowledge and discernment. I've included an appendix on page 133 with some resources that may be helpful both for individuals and groups that wish to study the issues further. Some of these resources have, on their web sites, specific prayer requests. Others are good sources for obtaining additional information on events in Israel. There are so many competing opinions and such a clamor of views that we need to ask God for discernment.

Finally, we should join the hymn writer Horatio Spafford in praying, "Lord, haste the day when my faith shall be sight"! Lord, we long for the day when You will

come to bring the ultimate peace to Jerusalem. Help us
to be men and women who are "looking for and has-
tening the coming of the day of God" (2 Peter 3:12)—
not through acts of violence, but through deeds of
kindness accompanied by a message of hope.

"JUST SOME BULLETS . . ."

One unintended consequence of Israel's ongoing struggle with terrorism is that it is one of the most security-conscious countries in the world. I learned just how much so during one of our student trips.

We were getting ready to fly home from Ben Gurion airport near Tel Aviv. Knowing Israel's strict security, we planned on arriving at the airport at least three hours before the flight. This required a 2:00 A.M. wake-up call in Jerusalem, with the bus departing for the airport at 3:00 A.M. It was so early that I forgot to explain to the students what to expect once we got to the airport. And I paid for that simple mistake.

We were checking in as a group. The normal procedure for groups is that the security personnel select the leader and one other participant—chosen at random—to take aside for questioning. The questions are fairly straightforward, but at 4:00 A.M. our minds aren't always functioning at peak efficiency. That's why I usually explain to the group what they will be asked, and why.

I knew the answers to the questions, but as I looked across the room at the other individual who had been selected, I saw we were in trouble. Under the intimidating conditions (which are part of the security process), he was "over-answering" the questions.

Question: "Has your luggage been in your sight since you packed it?" *Answer:* "No!" (He packed it, carried it to the bus himself, and loaded it under the bus. But it *was* out of sight while we drove to the airport!)

Question: "Did you meet anyone in Israel?" *Answer:* "Yes!" (He had met the bus driver, the guide, and the man who piloted the boat on the Sea of Galilee, even though he had not spent personal time alone with any of them.)

Question: "Did you ever leave the group and go off

alone?" *Answer:* "Yes!" (He went to the bathroom by himself, and he had done a little shopping in the Old City of Jerusalem.)

Question: "Do you have any weapons, or anything that could be used as a weapon?" *Answer:* "Just some bullets!" (On the Golan Heights he had found some bullets and thought they would make a great souvenir for his son. He hadn't bothered to tell anyone, but now that they were asking, he shared the information.)

Over two hours later, after our group had every suitcase, backpack, and piece of carry-on luggage opened and thoroughly searched, the last of us made it up to the gate just as the flight was beginning to board. America has gotten more security conscious, but you haven't seen security until you go through Ben Gurion airport! I'm thankful for the security. But if you are ever part of my group, don't pick up any bullets!

On another occasion a group of us were walking down Ben Yehuda Street in West Jerusalem on a Saturday evening. Shabbat had ended, and the street was full of people looking to enjoy a warm Saturday evening. Musicians stood at the street corners to entertain the passing crowds, collecting coins in their instrument cases.

As we approached one intersection, it seemed unusually crowded. Looking through the knot of people I saw a mime in the center of the street, trying to get out of his imaginary glass box. At that moment a bomb squad truck pulled onto Ben Yehuda street, its blue lights flashing. People, looking just a little nervous, stepped back to allow the van through. It turned at the corner where we were standing and stopped in front of a store. I could sense some tension in the crowd.

Just as the van was passing by, I happened to glance over at the mime. He remained completely in character. When the van reached him he raised his hands, arched his eyebrows, and mouthed the letter "O" in mock surprise. And as the van turned the corner in front of him, he became a traffic cop, waving the van through the intersection. The crowd burst into applause!

And the bomb? It turned out to be nothing more than a shopping bag left behind by a careless shopper. But Israel has learned that the only way to thwart terrorism is to maintain a constant state of vigilance.

OTHER VIEWS

Iraq's Christian History

Though many fled Saddam and sanctions in the '90s, more than 350,000 Christians have remained in Iraq. These men and women, who trace their church lineage to Pentecost, are caught in a clash between Eastern and Western powers that echos a conflict faced by their forefathers in the faith.

During the fourth century, Persia's ongoing conflict with the newly Christianized Roman Empire threatened to destroy the Christians living in the Mesopotamian lands of modern-day Iraq.

Mesopotamia emerged on the New Testament scene during Pentecost in Acts 2:9 when Luke noted the presence of Parthians from Mesopotamia. Soon the Gospel spread to Mesopotamia from Edessa, known today as Urfa, which is located in southeastern Turkey. Edessa was the Assyrian region's major trading center and became one of the early church's most successful missionary-sending cities. This Assyrian Church found great evangelistic success among the Mesopotamian Jews, who shared the Syriac language—a close relative of Jesus' own Aramaic mother tongue.

However, Mesopotamian Christians began suffering severe persecution from Persia following Constantine's conversion in 312 A.D. "After [Christianity's] adoption by Constantine, it was regarded by the Persian rulers as the faith of their deadliest rivals," says Yale historian Kenneth Scott Latourette. Christians were accused of aiding Rome and opposing the dominant philosophy of Zoroastrianism—a cult that did not look favorably on competing religions.

Latourette's final assessment may give some comfort to the modern heirs of those beleaguered fourth-century believers: "The amazing fact is not that Christianity remained a minority cult, but that it survived at all."

Collin Hansen, Christianity Today online, 02/07/03

Tour of Saddam's Palace

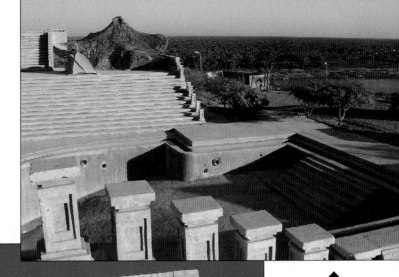

▲
Palace swimming
pool overlooking
Euphrates River

◀ Palace exterior

Details of interior
decoration
▼

▲
Procession Street walls (1987)

Procession Street walls (2003)
▼

The Saddam Hussein Guest House

▲
Exterior shot (1987)

Interior shot (2003)
▼

Camp Babylon, Iraq (2003)

Multinational force based at Babylon

▲ Model of Ishtar Gate (1987)   ▲ Ishtar Gate (2003)

Old and New Together

Hussein's palace dominates the remains of ancient Babylon.

▲ View of Nebuchadnezzar's palace from Hussein's palace

Satellite image by SpaceImagingEurasia

Multinational force's
equipment parked ▶
by theater

Return to Babylon after the War

Hussein's palace on the hill ▶

Satellite image by SpaceImagingEurasia

◀ Nebuchadnezzar's palace from the air

Looking down the Procession Street

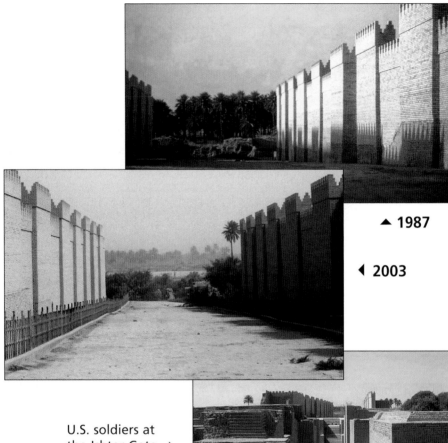

▲ 1987

◀ 2003

U.S. soldiers at
the Ishtar Gate ▶
(2003)

◀ Looking across
the Ishtar Gate
to the Ninmach
Temple

6
The Last Act

While they are saying, "Peace and safety!" then destruction will come upon them suddenly like labor pains upon a woman with child, and they will not escape.

1 Thessalonians 5:3

"You will be hearing of wars and rumors of wars. See that you are not frightened, for those things must take place, but that is not yet the end."

Matthew 24:6

It's hard to imagine a time when Israel and the Palestinians will be at peace. But that is precisely what will happen, according to the Bible. It won't be an American president who intervenes; it will be someone from Europe who finally "solves" the problem. He will broker an agreement that will seem, at last, to bring harmony, stability, and prosperity to this strife-torn region.

So will that make Islamic fundamentalism go away?

Unfortunately, it will not. Any Israeli-Palestinian peace treaty will require the Palestinians to grant Israel a right to exist in the land. And that is something Islamic fundamentalists will not accept. If we read Ezekiel

38–39, we see a prediction of an attack on Israel. The prophet presents the panoramic outline of what could be the response of Islamic fundamentalism to this treaty.

"After many days you will be summoned; in the latter years you will come into the land that is restored from the sword, whose inhabitants have been gathered from many nations to the mountains of Israel which had been a continual waste; but its people were brought out from the nations, and they are living securely, all of them. You will go up, you will come like a storm; you will be like a cloud covering the land, you and all your troops, and many peoples with you" (Ezekiel 38:8–9).

Ezekiel continues, speaking the word of the Lord he had received: "Therefore prophesy, son of man, and say to Gog, 'Thus says the Lord God, "On that day when My people Israel are living securely, will you not know it? You will come from your place out of the remote parts of the north, you and many peoples with you, all of them riding on horses, a great assembly and a mighty army"'" (vv. 14–15).

This passage describes a time when Israel seems finally to be at peace. It is during that time of peace that Israel will be invaded by attackers from Magog, Put, Cush, Persia, Beth-togarmah—real countries in Ezekiel's time, mentioned as early as Genesis 10. Magog was between the Black and Caspian Seas. Persia, of course, is Iran; Cush was the region just south of Egypt, modern-day Sudan; Togarmah was in the Armenian area. Put is Libya.

If we overlay these ancient regions over a contemporary map (see p. 100), we make an interesting discovery.

They all match up with areas that today are either dominated by Islamic fundamentalism or struggling with it. Along the southern edge of Russia you have the breakaway Islamic republics, including Chechnya, which continues to be an area of conflict. Turkey is officially a secular country, but the party in power has its roots in Islamic fundamentalism. Iran we know about all too well. And both Sudan and Libya are ruled by fundamentalist Muslims.

Letting the Guard Down

The prophet Daniel writes that this final period of time begins when the coming ruler from the West makes "a firm covenant with the many" for a seven-year period of time (Daniel 9:27). Who are "the many"? It could be many within Israel, or it could refer to many nations. One dangerous element of the conflict between Israel and the Palestinians is that its impact extends well beyond the boundaries of their land. It has repercussions for Egypt, Jordan, Lebanon, Syria, Saudi Arabia, and even Iraq. These other countries have large Palestinian populations, many living in refugee camps. The third holiest site in all Islam is in Jerusalem. And other political and religious factions within these countries have tried to use the conflict to gain popular support.

Any lasting agreement between Israel and the Palestinians will also involve these other countries. In what seems to be a stroke of brilliance, this future European leader will broker a multinational peace agreement—one that seems to "solve" the Middle East crisis. From

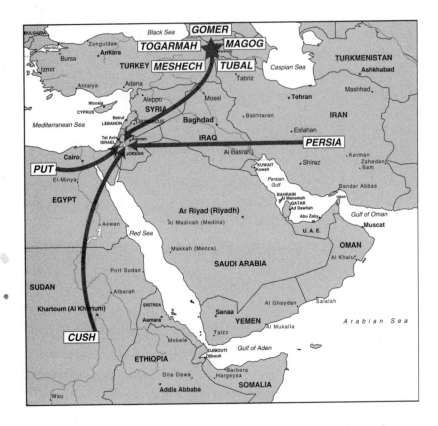

Iraq to Egypt, from Syria and Lebanon to Saudi Arabia, this will be a comprehensive peace encompassing Israel, the Palestinians, and all their near neighbors. After decades of war, peace will finally seem to be at hand in the Middle East. Israel's weary but joyful response is, "Finally! At last we can turn our 'swords into plowshares' and focus on economic growth instead of national security. Our borders are finally secure!"

Israel may be at peace with her near neighbors. But other, more fundamentalist Islamic countries will react violently to the treaty as they say to their Arab cousins, "You can't do that. You have just violated God's law in the Quran. You've given away what can't be given away, and you have done so to the cursed Jews!" They will begin to plot and conspire, and they will finally take matters into their own hands and launch a surprise attack against "those who are at rest, that live securely, all of them living without walls and having no bars or gates" (Ezekiel 38:11). That's Israel.

Ezekiel tells us, though, that this invasion is defeated . . . by God. The way the prophet describes the battle suggests that God Himself intends to use the war to show Israel that He alone is God. "'It will come about on that day, when Gog comes against the land of Israel,' declares the Lord God, 'that My fury will mount up in My anger. In My zeal and in My blazing wrath I declare that on that day there will surely be a great earthquake in the land of Israel'" (Ezekiel 38:18–19). The ultimate "act of God"—a devastating earthquake at the precise time these invaders reach Israel—stops the armies in their tracks. But God is not done. The prophet goes on to describe the other means God will use to stop these invaders.

God will use the confusion of the earthquake to confound the invading armies so that "every man's sword will be against his brother" (Ezekiel 38:21). In other words, these groups start fighting among themselves. It isn't too speculative a leap to imagine the battlefield chaos caused by the Iranians speaking Farsi, the Turks speaking Turkish, the southern Russians speaking Russian, and the Libyans and Sudanese speaking Arabic. The confusion caused by the earthquake is multiplied by the babble of tongues of these invaders.

As we look back over our recent conflicts in Afghanistan and Iraq, we see the instances of "friendly fire"—times when, in the confusion of battle, we mistake friends for foes. And if the United States with its sophisticated communications equipment suffers from friendly fire, imagine the scene when a multinational, multiethnic army, speaking a variety of native tongues, launches an attack that is suddenly disrupted by a severe earthquake. In the panic and confusion, the different elements target themselves by mistake.

But God doesn't end there. "With pestilence and with blood I shall enter into judgment with him; and I shall rain on him and on his troops, and on the many peoples who are with him, a torrential rain, with hailstones, fire and brimstone" (Ezekiel 38:22). Plague decimates the troops; hailstones rain down—and because of the earthquake, there is no shelter, nothing to hide under. "Burning sulfur" might describe a volcanic eruption on the Golan Heights, which is dotted with extinct volcanoes. God seems to choose this precise point in time to awaken those mountains from their ancient slumber.

God concludes: "I shall magnify Myself, sanctify Myself, and make Myself known in the sight of many nations; and they will know that I am the LORD" (v. 23). The effects of the battle will have international repercussions.

A Crisis of Faith

With the destruction of this multinational army of Islamic fundamentalists, the Islamic world will face a crisis of faith. Their defeat will not have come at the hands of a superior military force. Their attack will catch both Israel and the European leader by surprise. It is God Himself who blunts and then crushes the invaders. This attack, launched under the banner of Islamic conquest, will incur the displeasure of heaven. And as God turns against the Muslim fundamentalists, their stunning defeat will end their threat once and for all.

In contrast, the Jews will come to the realization that their nation was just delivered from certain destruction by the hand of God. The new European leader, the one who brokered the peace treaty that supposedly made Israel safe, did nothing. A national religious awakening begins to take hold in Israel as the Jewish people turn back to the true God. Sometime later the leader from Europe returns to Israel and, according to the apostle Paul, "takes his seat in the temple of God, displaying himself as being God" (2 Thessalonians 2:4). But when he demands, "I'm God, worship me," Israel says, "No, you're not." Why? Because they just witnessed the power of their true God at work.

But the Muslim fundamentalists, who were so convinced that God was on their side, are in absolute confusion. God has turned against them! Were they mistaken? What now? Perhaps this European leader has some answers. When this leader appears to die and rise again from the dead, they turn to him as a new prophet. "And they worshiped the beast, saying, 'Who is like the beast, and who is able to wage war with him?'... And authority to act for forty-two months was given to him" (Revelation 13:4–5).

It's important to add here that when we hear of "the world" following this future leader from Europe, we need to read that in its overall context. Not every single person in the world will follow him during the forty-two months of his quest to conquer the earth. Many in Israel will eventually reject his claims of authority. But for a period of three and a half years he will appear to have "authority over every tribe and people and tongue and nation" (Revelation 13:7).

"The King of the North"

The book of the prophet Daniel also includes an amazingly detailed account of the battles of the last days, and Israel's role in those battles:

"At the end time the king of the South will collide with him, and the king of the North will storm against him with chariots, with horsemen and with many ships; and he will enter countries, overflow them and pass through. He will also enter the Beautiful Land, and many countries will fall; but these will be rescued out of his hand: Edom, Moab and the foremost of the sons of Ammon. Then he will stretch out his hand against other countries, and the land of Egypt will not escape. But he will gain control over the hidden treasures of gold and silver and over all the precious things of Egypt; and Libyans and Ethiopians will follow at his heels. But rumors from the East and from the North will disturb him, and he will go forth with great wrath to destroy and annihilate many. He will pitch the tents of his royal pavilion between the seas and the

beautiful Holy Mountain; yet he will come to his
end, and no one will help him."
Daniel 11:40–45

The "Beautiful Land" refers to Israel; the "king of the
North" is this end-time ruler from Europe. Though God
will destroy the invading Muslim forces that try to
attack Israel (Ezekiel 38–39), this ruler will himself
begin assembling an army of conquest. Their staging
ground will be Israel—the Beautiful Land. In the book
of Revelation the apostle John identified the specific
spot where this army of conquest begins to assemble—
in the broad Valley of Jezreel near the hill of the ancient
city of Megiddo. "And they gathered them together to
the place which in Hebrew is called Har-Magedon" (Revelation 16:16).

"Armageddon" is often used as the symbolic name
for the final battle of the ages. But the book of Revelation actually pictures it as the staging area from which
the final military campaign *starts,* not where the last
battle *ends.*

When we compare the ancient countries named in
Daniel 11 to today, we have some idea of how each of
them will fare in the battles to come. (See map on page
112.) Edom, Moab, and Ammon, for example, occupied the land that is today modern Jordan. Daniel seems
to indicate that Jordan will be something of a safe haven
for Israelis during the coming time of persecution. Egypt,
Libya, and the "Nubians"—that is, the black Africans
south of Egypt—won't fare so well. The European leader
will invade Africa.

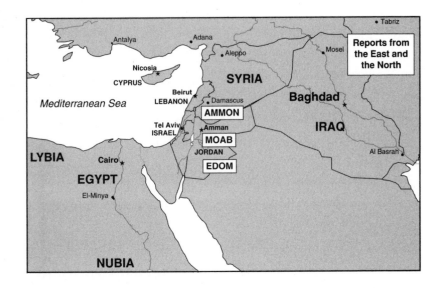

But then, "rumors from the East and from the North" will alarm him (v. 44). Where's that? Daniel's focus of direction was always Jerusalem. He prayed toward Jerusalem (Daniel 6:10), and his references to the king of the North and king of the South describe nations that were, from a Jewish perspective, geographically north and south of Jerusalem (Daniel 11). When Daniel describes this ruler receiving disturbing news "from the East and from the North," we need to look east and north of Jerusalem—presumably somewhere toward Iraq. Daniel doesn't say specifically where, so we must be careful not to resort to the fill-in-the-blanks sort of temptation that some can fall prey to and become too dogmatic. But it is plausible that this European ruler could have received disturbing news from Babylon and Iraq, which are north and east of Jerusalem.

As we've already discussed, eventually a strong ruler will rebuild Iraq, with the cooperation of the European nations, and get the oil flowing. In Revelation 17 the apostle John describes an alliance between the "woman," Babylon, and a "beast," this European leader and his group of allies. What's more, John indicates that the ruler and his allies "will hate the harlot and will make her desolate and naked, and will eat her flesh and will burn her up with fire" (17:16). What type of report could so upset this ruler that he diverts his forces to launch such a vicious attack?

Perhaps he receives word that Babylon has cut off his oil supply. Without oil, his tanks and ships and planes —his entire military machine—grinds to a halt. Perhaps Babylon and her other Arab allies formed a new alliance to oppose this leader's attack against fellow Arab nations in North Africa. God doesn't tell us the exact reason, but He does indicate that the news "from the East and from the North" was unexpected and unwelcome.

An End, and a Beginning

The armies of the European leader destroy Babylon. While the merchants on earth mourn the loss of revenue (Revelation 18:9–19), heaven rejoices (vv. 20–24). After crushing Babylon, the evil ruler returns to his original plans for conquest. And the center of the bull's-eye is Israel and Jerusalem. "He will pitch the tents of his royal pavilion between the seas and the beautiful Holy Mountain" (Daniel 11:45). The last battle in the campaign of Armageddon will take place in the hill country of Judah, at the city of Jerusalem. "For I will gather all the nations against Jerusalem to battle" (Zechariah 14:2).

Then comes the final confrontation, described in both the Old and New Testaments. "Then the Lord will go forth and fight against those nations, as when He fights on a day of battle. And in that day His feet will stand on the Mount of Olives, which is in front of Jerusalem on the east; and the Mount of Olives will be split in its middle from east to west by a very large valley, so that half of the mountain will move toward the north and the other half toward the south" (Zechariah 14:3–4). God's "road map for peace" goes right through the Mount of Olives!

> "And I saw heaven opened, and behold, a white horse, and He who sat on it is called Faithful and True, and in righteousness He judges and wages war. His eyes are a flame of fire, and on His head are many diadems; and He has a name written on Him which no one knows except Himself. He is clothed with a robe dipped in blood, and His name is called The Word of God. And the armies which are in heaven, clothed in fine linen, white and clean, were following Him on white horses. From His mouth comes a sharp sword, so that with it He may smite the nations, and He will rule them with a rod of iron; and He treads the wine press of the fierce wrath of God, the Almighty. And on His robe and on His thigh He has a name written, 'KING OF KINGS, AND LORD OF LORDS'" (Revelation 19:11–16).

Massed against this Rider from heaven are "the beast and the kings of the earth and their armies," pausing from their assault against Jerusalem to fight against the forces of heaven. But the battle of the ages is quite anti-climactic. "And the beast was seized . . . and the rest were killed with the sword which came from the mouth of Him who sat on the horse" (Revelation 19:19–21).

And it all happens in the Beautiful Land!

BUT ISN'T ALL THIS SYMBOLIC?

Bible prophecy has gotten a bad name in some quarters. It's associated with religious fringe sects who went out and sat on hills waiting for the end of the world, or elaborate charts linking current figures and events with the end times. Even Christians who take the Bible seriously wonder if they can understand many of the prophetic references in Scripture beyond the most obvious generalizations. After all, they say, if it were really clear, wouldn't more Christians agree on the interpretation?

We can respond to these questions two ways. First, we need to challenge the assumption that "it isn't true unless everybody agrees." Think, for example, of Martin Luther. The recent movie about him, *Luther,* powerfully showed how he stood nearly alone against the church of his day, protesting the indulgences commonly paid to grease the way to heaven. In Luther's day the vast majority of Christendom disagreed with *sola fides*—the doctrine that we are saved by faith alone. And they said, "The world's against you, Martin Luther." And Luther said, "Well, then, Luther is against the world." Truth is not a democracy. Ultimate truth resides in the true text of Scripture.

Second, we need to challenge the assumption that prophecy is too difficult to interpret. And the way to do this is to look at examples of prophecy from the Bible itself.

Reading Between the Lines

How then do we interpret the text?

The best approach is to look at past prophecy that was fulfilled. And the preeminent examples of that are the Old Testament prophecies of the Messiah. The prophet Micah wrote, "But as for you, Bethlehem Ephra-thah, too little to be among the clans of Judah, from you One will go forth for

Me to be ruler in Israel. His goings forth are from long ago, from the days of eternity" (Micah 5:2).

Bethlehem? Bethlehem was a small, out-of-the-way place in Micah's day. Reading further, the prophecy seems to say that even though the Messiah is going to be born in Bethlehem, He has already existed. Both of these elements were fulfilled in the birth of Jesus Christ. Mary became pregnant, and she and Joseph had to travel to their ancestral home of Bethlehem for the Roman census. While there, Jesus was born, thus fulfilling the prophecy—exactly as written.

The prophet Zechariah acted out a message intended to predict Israel's rejection of her God-appointed Shepherd. The Shepherd would only be valued at thirty pieces of silver (Zechariah 11:12). And those pieces would be thrown into the temple to buy a potter's field (11:13). Judas betrayed Jesus for thirty pieces of silver and threw the money into the temple. The money was then used to purchase the Potter's Field as a place of burial (Matthew 27:3–10)—exactly as written.

Zechariah also prophesied the Messiah would ride into Jerusalem on a colt, the foal of a donkey (Zechariah 9:9), and Jesus did just that (Matthew 21:1–5). And Isaiah the prophet announced the coming of a "Suffering Servant." "Surely our griefs He Himself bore, and our sorrows He carried; yet we ourselves esteemed Him stricken, smitten of God, and afflicted. But He was pierced through for our transgressions, He was crushed for our iniquities; the chastening for our well-being fell upon Him, and by His scourging we are healed" (Isaiah 53:4–5). Philip the evangelist explained to an Ethiopian official that this passage described the work of Jesus on the Cross (Acts 8:26–35)—exactly as written.

"Well, but Jesus is the exception," someone might argue. "Show me another example of prophecy that was fulfilled exactly as written."

Around 700 B.C. the prophet Isaiah told King Hezekiah

of Judah that the nation would be taken into captivity in Babylon (Isaiah 39:5–7). This event didn't take place until 586 B.C.—over a century after Isaiah penned the words. But the prophet was so certain of the outcome of his message that he began in Isaiah 40 to write to those people who would eventually be taken into captivity. He announced to them wonderful news. They would be rescued from Babylon by Cyrus, the great Persian king who conquered Babylon in 539 B.C. and allowed the various captive nations to return home.

Cyrus was not a believer in God, but God used him, exactly as Isaiah predicted.

> "Thus says the Lord to Cyrus His anointed, whom I have taken by the right hand, to subdue nations before him and to loose the loins of kings; to open doors before him so that gates will not be shut: . . . I will give you the treasures of darkness and hidden wealth of secret places, in order that you may know that it is I, the Lord, the God of Israel, who calls you by your name. For the sake of Jacob My servant, and Israel My chosen one, I have also called you by your name; I have given you a title of honor though you have not known Me. I am the Lord, and there is no other; besides Me there is no God." (Isaiah 45:1, 3–5)

Judah's release from captivity through a man named Cyrus happened exactly as God predicted through Isaiah—160 years before the event.

God gave the prophecy of Cyrus, and God fulfilled that prophecy exactly as written. That has been God's pattern throughout history. Why would God make such predictions? Because He—and nobody else—can! "I am the Lord, that is My name; I will not give My glory to another, nor My praise to graven images. Behold, the former things have come to pass, *now I declare new things; before they spring forth I proclaim them to you*" (Isaiah 42:8–9, italics added). "Thus says the Lord, the King of Israel and his Redeemer, the Lord of hosts: 'I am the first and I am the last, and there is no God besides Me. Who is like Me? Let him proclaim and declare it; yes, let him recount it to Me in order, from the time that I established the ancient nation. *And let them declare to them the things that are coming and the events that are going to take place*'" (Isaiah 44:6–7, italics added).

We can trust that God will do what He says He will do. In everything that led up to the first coming of Christ, the events unfolded the way He said they would, and we need to expect that the events leading up to His second coming will unfold as God says they will. God is faithful. His Word can be trusted.

And Israel's being back in the land after two thousand years is the beginning of that final sequence of events.

Simplistic vs. Simple

Having said that, it is important to make a distinction between what's simplistic and what's simple. The danger in prophecy—and it is a temptation some Christians have succumbed to—is to construct simplistic models that try to fill in all the gaps and to force current events into Bible prophecy. For example, during World War II some were identifying Hitler as the Anti-christ, Japan as the "kings from the east," and Mussolini as the false prophet. On a simplistic level, it looked good . . . until Mussolini was killed, Hitler committed suicide, and Japan was defeated.

Such misguided predictions—along with a fill-in-the-blanks view of prophecy—have occurred in almost every generation. The intentions have been good, arising out of a longing for Christ's return, but in their zeal to have this be the final generation, some have led astray those who desperately want to understand Bible prophecy.

God didn't fill in all the details of everything that's going to happen. He left large gaps. So as we explore what the Bible says about God's program for the future, in faith and trust, we need to approach the topic with a sense of humility that says, "This much we know—and this, frankly, we do not know."

This we do know: God holds the future—and He can be trusted.

OTHER VIEWS

"Yes, I am worried about a big attack. That is what they [terrorists who have flocked to Baghdad] specialize in. You study Al Qaeda, and that's what they are good at. They . . . think . . . that if you kill enough Americans in a big attack, we'll go away."

—**Paul Bremer,** U.S. civilian administrator in occupied Iraq, quoted by James O'Shea in *Chicago Tribune,* 10/19/03

"If the Bush Administration is able to seize this moment and provide American leadership that actually results in a stable and peaceful resolution between Israel and Palestine, I think that almost all of America's evangelicals will praise him."

Christianity Today editor David Neff, at a news conference of religious leaders urging support of the Bush "roadmap"
(*New York Times,* 12/06/03)

7
Two Friends of Mine

A generation goes and a generation comes, but
the earth remains forever. . . . That which has
been is that which will be, and that which has
been done is that which will be done. So there is
nothing new under the sun.

Ecclesiastes 1:4, 9

Samuel, the land operator I work with in Israel,
is a Jewish believer whose father came to Israel from
Morocco in the early 1950s, shortly after Israel achieved
independence. His grandfather had been killed by the
Nazis. When Samuel's father first came to faith in Jesus
as his Messiah, his mother said, "The Christians got
your father and now they've got you." She sent him to
the rabbi—they were still in Morocco—and the rabbi
said, "Your problem is you don't know Hebrew. If you
went to Israel and learned Hebrew, you'd realize why
Christianity is wrong for the Jews."

So Samuel's father immigrated to Israel, a young
man in a young country, and he learned Hebrew. Rather

than turning him against Jesus, learning Hebrew convinced him all the more of his faith, and he became a fearless and tireless witness for Jesus. He started one of the first Messianic congregations in Israel at a time when there were only a handful of Jewish believers in the country. He became a bold evangelist, starting his own publishing company to disseminate Christian literature.

But the building in which his congregation met was attacked and firebombed; his car was firebombed. His son, my travel agent friend, at times needed a police escort to go back and forth from school—to protect him from being attacked by Orthodox Jews, who were also behind the other assaults.

But the violence didn't stop my friend's dad. He has served his Messiah for over forty years. And he's as passionate as ever.

So is his son. They're both passionate for Jesus as the Messiah; and they believe Jews need to hear the message. But they're also deeply committed to the State of Israel.

Shaban the Ex-Terrorist

I know a man who's a shopkeeper in the Old City. No, not Murphy, whom we met earlier—this man is Murphy's brother. His name is Shaban; he's a devout Muslim whose father-in-law is one of the religious leaders appointed to serve at the Dome of the Rock.

Though he is growing more dignified with age, as a young man Shaban looked like our image of a terrorist

—lanky, bearded, with a broken tooth and dark, passionate eyes. He *was* a member of the PLO and was jailed for several years for his activities. Now, though, he's more mature, married with a family. Over the years as I've taken my student groups to Israel, we've done a lot of business with Shaban and Murphy, and I've built up a friendship. Shaban is a delightful guy to get to know.

One time I took my father to Israel. Dad knew the Middle East primarily through what he saw on the evening news, and as a result he felt uneasy for much of the trip. It was almost as if he were always looking over his shoulder for terrorists, because, as he said, "I don't trust Ishmael's children." The situation in Israel as presented in the media had made it seem as if Ali Baba and the Forty Thieves were going to jump out from a dark alley and attack at any time. The irony was that Shaban's shop is named the Ali Baba Souvenir Shop. So I just knew how Dad would react when I took him to meet Shaban.

Shaban, for his part, was deeply honored to meet my father. He grabbed one of his stools, cleaned the junk off, and set it down so Dad could have a place to sit. Then he sent a worker to a nearby shop to get Dad something to drink. Finally he said, "Let me give you a present!" He gave my dad a two-thousand-year-old "widow's mite" coin as a token of respect.

My father, of course, was relishing all this attention from his new friend. As we left he exclaimed, "What a nice guy!" I grinned. "You know, Dad, he was jailed for several years as a PLO terrorist." My dad's expression was priceless. He thought he knew what a terrorist was, and this nice shopkeeper did not fit the mold.

Shaban probably represents the majority of Muslims in Israel. He's devout; he probably wishes Israel would go away, but he's not so devout that he's dedicated to its destruction. He assumes Allah will take care of Israel in his time. In the meantime, he says, "Look, if an Israeli walks into my shop and wants to do business, I'm here to sell to him." It's one of those contradictions you find all over the Middle East.

Shaban would take my student groups on an "unauthorized" one-day tour of the West Bank, hiring an Arab bus with the required green license plates. About a half-mile past the Jewish checkpoint we would arrive at a Palestinian village on the West Bank, and Shaban would drape PLO flags over the front of the bus and transform it into a sort of PLO-mobile. It was bizarre, but it worked. We got stoned twice by little kids, but Shaban jumped out and screamed to them in Arabic. The stone throwing stopped, and he climb back onto the bus and proclaimed, "I am Shaban; I'm famous here!"

We went to Nablus, which is one of the hotbeds of Palestinian terrorist activity. Nablus is also where the biblical city of Shechem was located. The bus stopped, and we got out to walk to the current ruins. Suddenly a group of about twenty young men started to gather, eyeing us as if to say, *What are you doing here?* We began feeling a little nervous. But Shaban rattled off something in Arabic to them, and they ran to throw open the doors of their shops for us, showing us things to buy. "Shaban, what was all that about?" I asked.

"Well," he said, "when they saw you coming they

thought you were Jewish settlers. I just told them you were American tourists."

And that was that.

OTHER VIEWS

The Forgotten Palestinians

My father immigrated to America in the 1920s after his brother drowned in the Jerusalem quarry. People refused to help him, with Jews thinking he was Muslim, Muslims thinking he was Jewish, and Christians thinking he wasn't Christian.

There seems to be a growing detachment of Christians around the world from the plight of Palestinian Christians, who cling to their original roots, and who suffer harsh Israeli government oppression and occasional Muslim world bias.

. . . [Yet from] the seeds of a Nativity manger in tiny Bethlehem, a powerful religion arose. It is one story that, despite the hardships of the times, refuses to go away. And that remains a powerful inspiration to me.

Ray Hanania, a Christian Palestinian-American
The Daily Herald (Illinois), 12/1/03

The Fruit of Demonization

During [Ramadan], it is traditional in Arab/Muslim countries to broadcast special TV programming. Last year, Egypt broadcast a miniseries based on the anti-Semitic forgery the "Protocols of the Elders of Zion." This year, Hezbollah's channel broadcast a Syrian series, "The Diaspora," another program that relied on grotesque stereotypes alleging a Jewish plot to control the world.

If they didn't have such horrible consequences, these programs might be laughable. Yet recent events—the bombings of two Istanbul synagogues and an arson attack against a Parish Jewish school being just the latest outrages—prove what happens as a result of continual demonization.

Chaya Gil, an Israeli writer
The Daily Herald (Illinois), 12/1/03

An Open Door?

The *Akron Beacon Journal* reports that a group of more than 20 volunteers from the area planned to visit Iraq to distribute at least 10,000 Bibles written in Arabic, with the help of the Christian churches there. Iraq has a population of about 24.7 million people who speak Arabic and Kurdish. About 3 percent are Christian or "other"; 60 to 65 percent are Shiite Muslims and 32 to 37 percent are Sunni Muslims. Jon Hanna, one of the organizers, said there is an urgency about the mission to Iraq because there has not been an opportunity for Christians to enter Iraq with such openness in his lifetime and because experts predict that the door of opportunity to evangelize within the country will likely close within two years.

From the *Akron Beacon Journal,* 11/12/03

WHERE JESUS IS REAL

One of the places in the Holy Land where Jesus seems closest isn't, paradoxically, a "real" place—a location where actual events in the Bible occurred. Finding these "real" places can be difficult. Too often somebody's built a church over them, or they're buried under the layers of the centuries, or they just don't live up to what we've imagined. In discussions with officials from the Israel Government Tourist Office I like to describe evangelical Christians "as people of the Land and the Book." We want to visit the actual spots where the events of the Bible took place, and then we want to pause and read the Bible to visualize what it must have been like when the actual events happened.

The Church of the Holy Sepulchre is located over the place tradition says Jesus was crucified. Countless pilgrims have visited there. But for many, it's a big disappointment: dark and cramped, packed with shouting people from different traditions. Many walk out feeling spiritually empty and let down.

I like to take groups of pilgrims directly from the Church of the Holy Sepulchre to the Garden Tomb. The Garden Tomb is one of the spiritual highlights on our trips to Israel because it "looks the part." When we visit Calvary, we want to see a hill that looks like a skull. And next to the Garden Tomb is a hill that looks like a skull. We expect to find a garden nearby, and the Garden Tomb has a garden. And we want a tomb that's empty, and the focal point of the Garden Tomb is an empty tomb.

Unfortunately, the Garden Tomb is probably not the real tomb in which Jesus was placed, but it's a wonderful place to imagine how those events unfolded. The site is controlled by evangelical Anglicans from the British Isles who share the message from the Bible as they guide the groups through the garden. Along the way they say, "Here's why we think this is the place. But whether it is or not doesn't matter, because we don't worship the tomb; we worship the One who's no longer in the tomb. And whether this is the right tomb or not doesn't matter, because He has risen from the dead!"

And that's why, in my tours, I've stopped telling people, "Oh, by the way, this isn't the right spot." Because it's not the location that matters; it's the One who lived, died, and then rose again who truly makes all the difference.

8
What's Next . . . for You?

Jesus said to him, "I am the way, and the truth, and the life; no one comes to the Father but through Me."

John 14:6

He who testifies to these things says, "Yes, I am coming quickly." Amen. Come, Lord Jesus.

Revelation 22:20

Have you read any or all of the *Left Behind* books? Even if you haven't, you probably know that these novels deal with the adventures and spiritual journeys of a group of people left on Earth during her last days. The books, as you know, have sold something like 55 million copies, and it isn't just because they tell an entertaining story. The authors have received numerous letters from readers sharing how they or loved ones have been brought to faith in Christ through the message of the books.

The message is a simple one, and it is the message that concludes the book of Revelation:

> "Behold, I am coming quickly, and My reward is with Me, to render to every man according to what he has done. I am the Alpha and the Omega, the first and the last, the beginning and the end. . . ." The Spirit and the bride say, "Come." And let the one who hears say, "Come." And let the one who is thirsty come; let the one who wishes take the water of life without cost."
>
> **Revelation 22:12–13, 17**

While it's important to inform ourselves, understand the complexities of the Middle East, and even get to know "real people" there who struggle with many of the same things we do—while these things are important, where we will spend eternity and to whom we surrender our lives while on earth is immeasurably more important. As we reflect on what the Bible says about the final drama of history, the fact that Christ may come *at any time* should be a source of joy and hope for the believer—and a sobering reminder for those who have not yet placed their trust in Him.

It's so easy for most of us not to think about these matters of eternal significance, to assume that Earth is all there is, that we'll be here forever, and that Jesus is going to stay right where He is in heaven. But as some of the events taking place in the world start to look like what the Bible has foretold, each of us should prayerfully consider where, and in whom, we are putting our trust.

When God Reached Down

The Bible is preeminently a great story of God's

reaching down to humankind. The Old Testament chronicles the story of God's love of, judgment against, but ultimately faithfulness toward His covenant people—Israel. The New Testament tells of God stooping to walk among us in human form, in an area that most saw as nothing more than a quarrelsome backwater of the Roman Empire. The Bible shows us that since the beginning, humans have been going their own way, disobeying God. Why can't we ever seem to get it right? The Bible speaks plainly: "For all have sinned and fall short of the glory of God" (Romans 3:23).

There are teachers today who declare that we have it within ourselves to achieve fulfillment and inner peace. Yet such achievements are always temporary at best, never lasting. The ever-growing list of self-help guides to personal happiness is evidence to the fact that no one has ever been able to achieve lasting inner peace through his or her own efforts. So the search goes on, and we wonder what we're missing.

Only Christ can fill the emptiness. Only Christ can bridge the gap between us and God. When Jesus died on the cross at the base of a hill outside Jerusalem, He was paying the eternal penalty for the sins of humanity—the sins of you and me. The fact that God raised Him from the dead is proof that His payment was sufficient. And God has promised that we, too, can have victory over sin and death.

But we can't have that victory without surrender—a surrender where we place our trust in our eternal destiny into the hands of Jesus Christ as our Lord and Savior.

Taking the Next Step

Are you ready?

If you want Christ to come into your life, you must trust in what He already has done for you. You can place your life in His hands—and rest in that confidence—by praying a simple prayer like the following:

> Dear Lord, I know that my life is empty and lonely apart from You. I also know and believe that You sent Your Son, Jesus Christ, to earth to die on the cross to pay the penalty for my sin. I don't want to be separated from You. I want the abundant life that Christ promised. I want to put my life into His hands, love Him, serve Him, and someday (maybe soon!) live with Him forever.
>
> Please forgive me of my sin and give me eternal life because of what Your Son has done for me. In Christ's name I ask this. Amen.

If you just prayed this prayer in sincerity, welcome to the family—and to the greatest adventure you will ever experience, journeying with the Savior.

Begin reading the Bible to find out more about that adventure. The gospel of John is a good place to start, because it will introduce you more fully to Jesus. Start praying and sharing your deepest needs, fears, and desires with God. Don't worry about how to pray. Think of prayer as family time with your heavenly Father. He wants to hear from you about all the details of your life, large and small. And find and join a church made up of a group of people who have also made a commitment to Christ. Let them help you get to know Him better. The publisher of this book is also eager to assist you in learning more about the Christian life. For more information, turn to the back of this book.

From Head to Heart

If you are already part of God's family and have been so for some time, let me share a word of encouragement. I, like you, am a longtime believer. I love God's Word, and in my head I have believed that what God said about the past is true, what He said about our life today is true, and what He said about the future is true.

But *being there* in Israel and Iraq, experiencing, even in a small way, God's Story, moved my beliefs from my head to my heart. It's walking down the Mount of Olives and realizing Jesus stood on that same mountain and surveyed Jerusalem—and wept. And suddenly you're asking yourself, "Why am I not weeping?"

It's traveling to Iraq and walking down the main street in Babylon and having the incredible sudden sensation: I'm walking on the same stones that Daniel trod. These walls were here when the young Daniel was serving the king, when he faced toward the location of the temple in Jerusalem and prayed. Am I as dedicated in my life of devotion to God as Daniel?

Certainly I would encourage you to travel to the Holy Land for yourself, to experience the Story, hear the waves lapping against the shore of the Sea of Galilee, feel the desert sun beaming down through majestic palm trees, walk the streets of Jerusalem's Old City—and then to ponder what this place has meant to so many people for so many centuries.

But beyond that, I would encourage you to remember that we serve a *living* Savior and that we follow God's *living* Word. This is not dusty theory and precept. This is life itself—as the woman from Samaria found out when the Man from Judea stopped and asked her for a drink. Life: with Him.

Come, Lord Jesus!

6

Appendix: Sources for Additional Information

E-mail Resources

"Israel Update" is a monthly e-mail written by David Dolan and published/distributed by Christian Friends of Israel in Jerusalem. To subscribe free of charge to the e-mail version of the "Israel Update," follow these instructions:

Send an e-mail to: listproc@grmi.org

Leave the subject blank (or put an asterisk "*" for AOL)

In the body text area type: Subscribe IsraelUpdate (your name)

EXAMPLE: Subscribe IsraelUpdate John Doe

To unsubscribe, e-mail them at listproc@grmi.org and write: Unsubscribe cfi-ind

"Israel Update" has the same name as the e-mail resource above, but this one is a regular e-mail provided by the Consulate General of Israel, Chicago. The update includes specific information on events in Israel, including recent terrorist activities and Israel's response. This site provides excellent information that can help Christians understand—and respond intelligently to—some of the journalistic and diplomatic misinformation about Israel. To subscribe free of charge to this e-mail service, follow these instructions:

Send an e-mail to: contactus@chicago.mfa.gov.il and in the subject line write: **Subscribe**

To unsubscribe, e-mail them at contactus@chicago.mfa.gov.il and in the subject line write: **Unsubscribe**

The Simon Wiesenthal Center is an international organization that seeks to promote tolerance and combat anti-Semitism worldwide. They send out periodic world news updates via e-mail. To be placed on their list, visit their web site (http://www.wiesenthal.com).

Web Resources

The "Bridges for Peace" web site (www.bridgesforpeace.com) provides news, information on specific prayer requests, and tangible ways Christians can help Israel.

The "Christian Friends of Israel" web site (www.cfijerusalem.org) contains a weekly prayer guide and other helpful resources for concerned Christians.

The "Friends of Israel" web site (www.foigm.org) contains links to this organization and an online opportunity to sign up for *Israel, My Glory* magazine.

The "International Christian Embassy Jerusalem" web site (www.icej.org) provides a section on specific things Christians can do to be a blessing to Israel.

The "Israel Defense Forces" web site (http://idf.il/newsite/english/main.stm) provides background information, briefings, and reports on activities and actions undertaken by the Israel Defense Forces. This is a good source of information on what is happening in the current conflict.

The "Israel Ministry of Foreign Affairs" web site (www.israel.org/mfa/home.asp) contains news reports and other information that can help a Christian pray specifically for Israel.

The "Israel Ministry of Tourism" web site (www.go israel.com) provides specific information on how events in Israel affect tourists and tourism.

News Resources on the Web

The *Ha'aretz* web site (www.haaretzdaily.com) provides excellent news and information from Israel.

The *Jerusalem Post* web site (www.jpost.com) also provides excellent news and information from Israel.

Note especially the "latest news" updates that provide reports on breaking news stories.

The "Palestinian Media Watch" (www.pmw.org.il) provides English translations of key Palestinian speeches, articles, and messages to illustrate the disparity between what the Palestinian Authority says to the world media in English and what they broadcast and print to their own people in Arabic.

Voicing Your Concerns to Congress and the President

The "Congress.org" web site (http://congress.org) provides address and telephone information for the president, vice president, and all members of Congress. It also provides an option for you to send an e-mail message to these individuals.

Sɪɴᴄᴇ 1894, Moody Publishers has been dedicated to equip and motivate people to advance the cause of Christ by publishing evangelical Christian literature and other media for all ages, around the world. Because we are a ministry of the Moody Bible Institute of Chicago, a portion of the proceeds from the sale of this book go to train the next generation of Christian leaders.

If we may serve you in any way in your spiritual journey toward understanding Christ and the Christian life, please contact us at www.moodypublishers.com.

"All Scripture is God-breathed and is useful for teaching, rebuking, correcting and training in righteousness, so that the man of God may be thoroughly equipped for every good work."
—2 Tɪᴍᴏᴛʜʏ 3:16, 17

MOODY
PUBLISHERS

THE NAME YOU CAN TRUST

More from Charlie Dyer and Moody Publishers

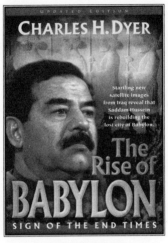

ISBN: 0-8024-0905-9

COULD OURS BE THE LAST GENERATION?

The Bible says Babylon—the mightiest city of the ancient world—will rise from its own ashes to play a vital role in the end times.

Regardless of what happens to Saddam Hussein, the Bible says Babylon will be rebuilt. And events are unfolding just as God's Word predicts. This compelling, timely book offers penetrating insights into the current Middle East crisis, biblical prophecy, and Babylon's place in last-day events.

MOODY
PUBLISHERS

THE NAME YOU CAN TRUST®

1-800-678-6928 www.MoodyPublishers.org

WHAT'S NEXT? TEAM

ACQUIRING EDITORS
William L. Thrasher, Jr. and Mark Tobey

DEVELOPMENT EDITOR
Elizabeth Cody Newenhuyse

BACK COVER COPY
Elizabeth Cody Newenhuyse

COVER DESIGN
Smartt Guys Design

COVER PHOTOS
CORBIS (Osama bin Laden)
Benjamin Lowy/CORBIS (soldier)
In Visu/CORBIS (Saddam Hussein statue)

INTERIOR DESIGN
Ragont Design

PRINTING AND BINDING
Dickinson Press, Inc.

The typeface for the text of this book is
Berkeley